THE IRISH RINGFORT

The Group for the Study of Irish Historic Settlement

The Group was founded in 1969 to encourage, co-ordinate and publish the study of Irish historic settlement, and to offer advice on matters relating to historic settlement which are of national and local concern. The Group achieves these aims through an annual weekend conference, com prising lectures and fieldtrips, focusing on a particular area, and through publication of an annual *Newsletter* and a regular series of scholarly monographs written by settlement experts. Membership and participation in the annual conference and fieldtrip is open to all. Further information may be obtained from www.irishsettlement.ie.

IRISH SETTLEMENT STUDIES

1 B.J. Graham, *Anglo-Norman settlement in Ireland* (1985). Out of print.
2 C.T. Cairns, *Irish tower houses: a Co Tipperary case study* (1987). Out of print.
3 R. Loeber, *The geography and practise of English colonisation in Ireland, 1534–1609* (1991); reprinted as R. Loeber, 'The geography and practice of English colonisation in Ireland 1534–1609' in R. Loeber (edited by K. Whelan and M. Stout), *Irish houses and castles 1400–1740*, (2019), pp 35–111.
4 B.J. Graham and L. Proudfoot, *Urban improvement in provincial Ireland, 1700–1840* (1994). Out of print.
5 M. Stout, *The Irish Ringfort* (1997)
6 P.J. Duffy, David Edwards and Elizabeth FitzPatrick (eds), *Gaelic Ireland c.1250–c.1650: land, lordship and settlement* (2001)
7 James Lyttleton and Tadhg O'Keeffe (eds), *The manor in medieval and early modern Ireland* (2005)
8 Elizabeth FitzPatrick and Raymond Gillespie (eds), *The parish in medieval and early modern Ireland: community, territory and building* (2006)
9 Linda Doran and James Lyttleton (eds), *Lordship in medieval Ireland: image and reality* (2007)
11 James Lyttleton and Colin Rynne (eds), *Plantation Ireland: settlement and material culture c.1550–c.1700* (2009)
12 Margaret Murphy and Matthew Stout (eds), *Agriculture and settlement in Ireland* (2015)
13 Bernadette Cunningham and Harman Murtagh (eds), *Lough Ree: historic lakeland settlement* (2015)
14 James Lyttleton and Matthew Stout (eds), *Church and settlement in Ireland* (2018)
15 Kevin Whelan, *Religion, landscape and settlement in Ireland: from Patrick to present* (2018)

Numbers 3, 5 and all subsequent numbers are available from Four Courts Press: www.fourcourtspress.ie.

Consulting Editor for *The Irish ringfort*
Professor Kevin Whelan, University of Notre Dame

Managing Editor for *The Irish ringfort*
Paul Ferguson, Trinity College Library, Dublin

IRISH SETTLEMENT STUDIES, NO. 5

The Irish Ringfort

Matthew Stout

FOUR COURTS PRESS

In association with the Group for the Study of Irish Historic Settlement

Published by
FOUR COURTS PRESS LTD
7 Malpas Street, Dublin 8, Ireland
www.fourcourtspress.ie
and in North America by
FOUR COURTS PRESS
c/o IPG, 814 N. Franklin Street, Chicago, IL, 60610.

A catalogue record for this title
is available from the British Library.

ISBN 978-1-85182-582-0

Printed in Ireland
by SprintPrint, Dublin

Contents

List of Illustrations

FIGURES

PLATES

TABLES

Dedicated to
my friend David Sweetman, 'our chief of men'

Acknowledgements

I wish to record my thanks to the following persons for their assistance in preparing this study: Professor F.H.A. Aalen, Professor John Andrews, Professor Desmond Gillmor, Mr Richard Haworth, Dr James Killen, Mr Martin Reinicke, Department of Geography, Trinity College Dublin; Mr John Bradley, Department of History, St Patrick's College, Maynooth; Professor Liam Breatnach, Department of Irish and Celtic Languages, Trinity College Dublin; Mr Victor Buckley, Mr Edward Bourke, Mr Muiris de Buitléir, Ms Sharon McMenamin, Ms Geraldine Stout, Mr David Sweetman, National Monuments Service, Department of Arts, Culture and the Gaeltacht; Ms Judith Carroll; Ms Beth Cassidy, ADS Ltd; Mr Mark Clinton; Dr Gabriel Cooney, Department of Archaeology, University College Dublin; Mr George Cunningham, Parkmore Press, Roscrea; Ms Felicity Devlin, National Museum of Ireland; Mr Charles Doherty, Department of History, University College Dublin; Mr David Doty, Rocky Mountains Conference Group, San Francisco; Ms Claire Foley, Dr Chris Lynn, Mr Brian Williams, Environment and Heritage Service, Department of Environment (NI); Ms Margaret Gowan; Mr Paul Ferguson, Map Library, Trinity College Dublin; Dr Finbar McCormick, Department of Archaeology, School of Geosciences, The Queen's University of Belfast; Mr Brian McDonald, Taighde (Research Ireland); Professor Frank Mitchell, Trinity College Dublin, Dr Michael Monk, Department of Archaeology, University College Cork; Dr Michael O'Connell, Department of Botany, University College Galway; Mr Gearóid Ó Riain, NRDC, Trinity College Dublin; Mr Jerry O'Sullivan, AOC Scotland Ltd; Dr Nerys Patterson, Department of Sociology, Harvard University; Mr Brian Redmond, The Photographers, Roscrea; Dr Michael Ryan, Chester Beatty Library; Professor Anngret Simms, Department of Geography, University College Dublin; Mr Leo Swan, ArchTech Ltd; and Professor Kevin Whelan, University of Notre Dame. I would especially like to thank Dr James Killen, Ms Geraldine Stout and Professor Kevin Whelan for their constant encouragement and for wading through the many earlier versions of this text.

Introduction

Our perceptions of Early Christian Ireland are dominated by the great ecclesiastical works of art and architecture: illuminated manuscripts like the Book of Kells; intricate metalwork like the Derrynaflan chalice; and works in stone such as the high crosses at Monasterboice. Furthermore, the view that during this golden age of Irish history Ireland was the 'isle of saints and scholars' again focuses popular attention on the monastic component of Irish settlement. These perceptions, however accurate, do not tell us much about the Early Christian landscape primarily because the majority of people in Ireland, then as now, were farmers and labourers rather than artists and priests. In this pre urban society, farmers created the wealth which sustained the monasteries. The upper echelons of that society, who ceded land and commissioned the great works of art, owed much of their status to the land and cattle each possessed. As it is my view that both high king and small farmer dwelt within the simple earthen or stone enclosures known collectively as ringforts, the study of this settlement form offers us our best chance to understand how all classes of secular society functioned during the Early Christian period in Ireland.

Although ringforts are by no means a neglected subject, geographers and archaeologists have not focused their attentions on them at a level merited by their sheer numbers. Ringforts are the most numerous archaeological monument found in Ireland and it is the only domestic monument which survives in significant numbers. As such they should have provided the raw material for analysis into the inner workings of Early Christian settlement. Unfortunately, many studies of ringfort distributions were used to support various theories of settlement continuity – spanning the Neolithic to the Middle Ages – all written before the narrow Early Christian date range of this monument type was fully appreciated. Many recent works examine distribution in a very superficial way, barely touching on the relationships between different types of ringforts.

The unspectacular nature of most ringforts must account for this relative neglect as well as a sense of inferiority which pervades early accounts of the settlement form. Richard Burton asked: 'If ancient Ireland were anything but savage where, let us ask, are the ruins that show any signs of civilisation? A people of artists does not pig in wooden shanties surrounded by a rude vallum of earthwork.[1] Pitt-Rivers, who accused nineteenth-century antiquarians of patterns; many of over-romanticising

---

1 Quoted in C. Costello, *Ireland and the Holy Land* (Dublin, 1974), p. 25.

the Gaelic past, claimed that they were 'bent on seeing in every hole and corner, which at every period of antiquity might have harboured a dog, vestiges of the departed and still fading splendour of the Emerald Isle'.[2] Evans, who seems to have internalised this attitude towards things Early Christian, attempted to push the clachan form of nucleated settlement – and the civilising effect of village life – back into the first millennium, thus diminishing the significance of dispersed settlement within ringforts.[3] The contribution which the study of ringforts can make to our understanding of Early Christian settlement and society has been passed over in many works; most notably in a historical geography of Early Christian Leinster which makes but a handful of references to ringforts,[4] and in a recent survey which offers only the briefest summary of the many significant contributions to ring fort studies.[5] Another index of the failure to adequately deal with this subject is evidenced by the fact that since the de Paor's masterly synthesis of Early Christian archaeology and society was published in the 1960s, the textbooks on settlement in this period have been written outside Ireland,[6] and only two doctoral theses have addressed the distribution of ringforts alone.[7]

This study is intended as a contribution towards an understanding of only one aspect of Early Christian settlement. While the content may appear overwhelmingly statistical, I am not apologetic about the need to quantify ringfort characteristics. Numbers underpin a solid descriptive foundation for ringforts, permit valid comparisons between morphological and literary references, allow for an accurate assessment of the physical determinants of settlement, and facilitate classification of ringfort type and regional variation. Only by first establishing what and where ringforts are (and are not) is it possible to look beyond this monument type to the society which built them in such great numbers.

This study examines the incontrovertible facts about ringforts; shape, size, date and function. It then deals with the nation-wide distribution of ringforts divided into areas on the basis of population density. In each area, earlier regional studies have been re-examined in the context of overall distribution between secular

---

2 Quoted in C. Lynn, 'Houses and other related outbuildings in Early Christian Ireland', unpublished PhD thesis, University College Dublin (1986), 3 vols; see vol. i, p. 23.   3 M. Stout, 'Emyr Estyn Evans and Northern Ireland: the archaeology and geography of a new state' in J. Atkinson, I. Banks and J. O'Sullivan (eds), *Nationalism and archaeology* (Glasgow, 1996), pp 111–27.   4 A. Smyth, *Celtic Leinster; towards an historical geography of Early Irish civilisation A.D. 500–1600* (Dublin, 1982).   5 D. Ó Cróinín, *Medieval Ireland 400–1200* (London, 1995).   6 M. de Paor and L. de Paor, *Early Christian Ireland* (London, 1961); N. Edwards, *The archaeology of Early Medieval Ireland* (London 1990); H. Mytum, *The origins of Early Christian Ireland* (London, 1992).   7 V. Proudfoot, 'Settlement and economy in county Down from the late Bronze Age to the Anglo-Norman invasions', unpublished PhD thesis (The Queen's University of Belfast, 1957); G. Barrett, 'The ring-fort: a study in settlement geography with special reference to southern county Donegal and the Dingle area, county Kerry', unpublished PhD thesis (The Queen's University of Belfast, 1972).

enclosures and ecclesiastical centres. Finally, the morphological and distributional characteristics are compared to written sources of the period. The people within ringforts are brought to the fore in this discussion, as is their relationship with neighbouring famisteads and religious communities. This study focuses on the lives and material remains of people who are often neglected in historical studies; the men and women who were not the kings and saints of official history, but rather farmers and herds and wives and children. We do not know their names, but they are not anonymous.

1 Morphology

The ringfort is such a common and simple monument, and one so familiar to Irish fieldworkers, that a definition seems almost unnecessary. Nonetheless, Ó Ríordáin's definition is provided here because it has a veracity forged during a life dedicated to fieldwork and archaeological survey. He described ring forts in the following terms:

> In its simplest form the ringfort may be described as a space most frequently circular, surrounded by a bank and fosse or simply by a rampart of stone. The bank is generally built by piling up inside the fosse the material obtained by digging the latter. Ringforts vary very considerably in size. In the more elaborately defended examples, the defences take up a much greater area than that of the enclosure.[1]

This definition briefly summarises the morphological characteristics – shape, size and variations – of this monument type, which arc now examined in greater detail.

Certainly, most ringforts are fairly circular. One method to quantify this derives an index of circularity by dividing a ringfort's minimum internal diameter by the maximum internal diameter, in which case 1.00 represents a true circle with descending values referring to less circular examples. Ringforts from the south-west midlands range from oval (0.56) to absolutely circular (0.99) with a mean of 0.88.[2] Sixty-five ringforts in north Roscommon had a mean circularity index of 0.92.[3] This means that a typical ringfort, with a maximum internal diameter of c.30m, would have a minimum internal measurement of c.27m. Damage and uneven spreading of the banks could account for the discrepancy from a true circle and it remains highly likely that the plan of each new ringfort was originally laid out using a measuring line pivoted from a central stake which could only have been accomplished on a greenfield site. It would be useful to know if oval or D-shaped sites show evidence

---

1 Ó Ríordáin, *Antiquities of the Irish countryside*, 5th ed. revised by R. de Valera (London, 1979), pp 29–30.   2 M. Stout, 'Ringforts in the south-west midland, of Ireland' in *Proceedings of the Royal Irish Academy*, xci (1991), C, pp 201–43; see p. 207, Throughout this paper the term 'south-west midlands' refers to the barony of lkerrin in north Tipperary and the barony of Clonlisk in south-west Offaly.   3 M. Keegan, 'Ringforts in north county Roscommon', unpublished BSc thesis (The Queen's University of Belfast, 1994), see p. 10.

for earlier occupation which would have prevented this reference to a central point when constructing the later ringfort. Constructing circular defences had practical and strategic advantages. Raising circular earthworks avoided the practical problem met by the architects of medieval moated sites; constructing a square enclosure resulted in the earth from two sides of an angle being thrown up onto the same point creating their diagnostic raised comers. The circular site also afforded broad perspectives of approaching attackers and allowed the maximum area to be enclosed relative to the length of bank constructed. Circularity was a feature of the model ringfort as described in the laws (see below, chapter 7) and perhaps links these sites and their occupants with the circular burial mounds of their pagan predecessors. The square enclosure was a Norman introduction,[4] and this imposed dichotomy in settlement forms in many ways mirrors the experience of native North Americans. Black Elk, forced to live in the rectangular homes built on government reservations, remarked that 'there can be no power in a square':

> You have noticed that every thing an Indian does is in a circle, and that is because the Power of the World always works in circles, and everything tries to be round ... the *Wasichus* have put us in these square boxes. Our power is gone and we are dying ...[5]

Spirituality may also have valued the advantages of a circular structure by suggesting that the corner of a dwelling was the likely haunt of the devil. The enclosed 'space' or living area of earthen ringforts ranges from internal diameters of 15.5m to 75m in the south-west midlands; 40% have internal diameters of between 28m and 35m. Ringforts with enclosed areas between 20m and 44m account for 84% of all surviving sites.[6] Comparable ranges of internal measurements have been found elsewhere in Ireland. 63% of ringforts in Monaghan have internal diameters of between 27m and 39m.[7] Ringforts tend to be smaller on the Iveragh peninsula where 56% of earthen and stone ringforts have internal diameters of between 20m and 30m.[8] More specifically, 23% of sites in north Kerry, 27% of sites in Donegal and 29% of sites in Ikerrin, Tipperary have modal internal diameters of between 27m and 31m.[9] As would be expected, the dimension given in the law tracts for

---

4 T. Barry, *Medieval moated sites of south-east Ireland* (Oxford, 1977).   5 J. Neihardt, *Black Elk speaks; being the life story of a holy man of the Oglala Sioux as told through John G. Neihardt (Flaming Rainbow)* (Lincoln, Nebraska, 1989); see pp 194–6. My thanks to David Doty and members of the Rockies Conference Group for help with this reference.   6 M. Stout, 'Ringforts in the south-west midlands', unpublished BA (mod.) dissertation (Trinity College Dublin, 1989); see table 1, pp 26–30; fig. 6a, p. 34.   7 A. Brindley, *Archaeological inventory of county Monaghan* (Dublin, 1986).   8 A. O'Sullivan and J. Sheehan, *The Iveragh Peninsula: an archaeological survey of South Kerry* (Cork, 1996), see pp 134–5.   9 C. Toal, North Kerry archaeological survey (Dingle, 1995); see p. 82; B. Lacy *et al.*, Archaeological survey of county Donegal (Lifford, 1983); G. Stout, *Archaeological survey of the barony of Ikerrin* (Roscrea, 1984), see p. 28.

the residence of a tribal king, namely 42.56m, lies in the upper range of ringfort diameters (see below, chapter 7).

Cashels, or stone-built ringforts, tend to be much smaller than earthen examples. The average earthen ringfort has an internal diameter of 22m in south Donegal, while cashels in the same area have an average internal diameter of 20m with half of them having internal diameters of between 15m and 24m. More striking, however, is the dimensional difference between stone and earthen ringforts in the west of the Dingle peninsula. Earthen ringfort internal diameters are 30m on average while cashels have a mean internal diameter of only 23m.[10] Further south in Kerry, on the Iveragh peninsula, cashels are on average 5m smaller than ringforts.[11] Many of the smaller cashels – occurring as they do in areas where stone walls are common and where the walls are more irregular and curvilinear than on better agricultural land – may be nothing more than small circular fields or cattle enclosures of no great antiquity. In the parish of Killasser, Mayo, there are six ringforts which have definite stone walls enclosed by, or enclosing, earthen banks.[12] It is not known how widespread the distribution of these hybrid, multivallate sites is.

Some ringforts, referred to as platform ringforts, have their interiors raised above the level of the surrounding countryside: 19% of sites in the south-west midlands are platform ringforts, and are raised an average of 1.43m above the surrounding ground level;[13] in Louth, 15% of ringforts have raised interiors with nineteen of the twenty-four examples raised over 2m above the surrounding ground surface.[14] Avery argues that a distinction should be made between ringforts whose interiors are slightly raised above ground level and 'prominent mounded sites'.[15] Excavations show that some ringforts served as the base for the high mounds, or mattes, built by the Normans in the earliest phases of their colonisation.[16] Despite this, low platform ringforts are rarely confused in the field with conical-shaped mattes. The recent excavations at Deer Park Farms, where one house was dated to AD648, is further confirmation of the Early Christian date of platform sites.[17] Lynn believes that the construction of a plat form created significant difficulties for the ringfort occupants, a greater effort was required to construct the enclosure, access became more difficult, internal structures were more exposed to weather conditions

10 Barrett, 'The ring-fort', table 6, pp 101–2.   11 O'Sullivan and Sheehan, *The Iveragh Peninsula*, p. 135.   12 B. O'Hara, *The archaeological heritage of Killasser, county Mayo* (Galway, 1991); see pp 115–16.   13 M. Stout, Ringforts, pp 207, 210.   14 V. Buckley and P. Sweetman, *Archaeological survey of county Louth* (Dublin, 1991), p. 152.   15 M. Avery, 'Caiseal na nDuini and Cashelreagan: two forts in Rosguill, county Donegal' in *Ulster Journal of Archaeology*, liv–lv (1991–2), pp 120–8; see p. 125. The problem arises as to what is 'prominent' and highlights the advantages of multivariate statistical techniques like cluster analysis which determine ringfort classifications on the basis of continuous data.   16 C. Lynn, 'The excavation of Rathmullan, a raised rath and motte in county Down' in *Ulster Journal of Archaeology*, xliv–v (1981-2), pp 65–171. A summary of excavated platform ringforts is provided in appendix 6.   17 C. Lynn, 'Deer Park Farms, Glenarm, county Antrim' in *Archaeology Ireland*, i (1987), pp 11–15.

and the site became more conspicuous and perhaps more prone to attack.[18] The most probable reason for taking on this extra effort and inherent disadvantage was almost certainly the need to elevate many sites above the water table. G. Stout has shown that platform ringforts are more common in low-lying positions in Ikerrin barony in Tipperary[19] and the same has been found in Small County barony in Limerick.[20] The water logging, which was such a boon to archaeologists at Deer Park Farms, was undoubtedly a nuisance for its original inhabitants. Raising the interior may have been an effort to eliminate these waterlogged conditions.

Ringforts are usually enclosed and defended by a single bank. Univallate ringforts, as they are known, account for over 80% of sites in most areas: 90% of sites were univallate in Morgallion barony, Meath; 88% in parts of Leitrim (OS 1:10560 sheets 12, 27 and 33); 88% in north Kerry; 85% in the Braid and Upper Glenarm valleys, Antrim; 83% in southern Donegal; 82% at Cruachain, Roscommon; 81% in the south-west midlands; 76% on the Iveragh peninsula in Kerry; and 69% in Louth.[21] After over a thousand years of denudation, these banks cannot be expected to display their original characteristics. In the southwest midlands, banks occasionally exceeded 2m in height, but surviving banks average only 0.48m, much lower than the value of 1.83m given for the bank height of a royal ringfort (see below chapter 7). In contrast, the width of surviving banks exceeds the original width due to settlement and spreading. On average, ringfort banks are now over 3m wide, that is larger than the 2.13m bank width provided for in the law tracts (see below, chapter 7).

As Ó Ríordáin has noted, the ditch or fosse of a ringfort served a dual function: it provided the material for the inner bank and, more important, it added to the site's defence. Not all ringforts have evidence for a fosse, but this is more likely due to their becoming filled in later than to an original absence. Only 3% of ringforts lack an outer fosse in north Roscommon, while 36% of ringforts lack any evidence for an outside fosse in the south-west midlands.[22] In Louth the figure is 43% and

18 Lynn, 'Rathmullan', p. 149. **19** G. Stout, *Ikerrin*, p. 26. **20** M. O'Kelly, 'A survey of antiquities in the barony of Small County, county Limerick; part I' in *North Munster Archaeological Journal*, iii (1942), pp 75–97; see p. 89. **21** N. Brady, 'An analysis of the spatial distribution of early historic settlement sites in the barony of Morgallion, county Meath', unpublished BA dissertation (University College Dublin, 1983), see p. 7 (n = 61); J. Farrelly, 'A sample study of ringforts in county Leitrim', unpublished MA thesis (University College Dublin, 1989), see p. 86 (n = 120); Toal, *North Kerry*, p. 82 (n = 351); L. Black, 'Early Christian settlement in the Braid and Upper Glenarm valleys', unpublished BA thesis (The Queen's University of Belfast, 1994), see p. 14 (n = 78); G. Barrett, 'A field survey and morphological study of ring-forts in southern county Donegal' in *Ulster Journal of Archaeology*, xliv (1980), pp 39–51 (n = 144); M. Herity, 'A survey of the royal site of Cruachain in Connaught Ill: Ringforts and ecclesiastical sites' in *Journal of the Royal Society of Antiquaries of Ireland*, 117 (1987), pp 125–41, see p. 128 (n = 119); M. Stout, 'Ringforts', p. 207 (n = 201); O'Sullivan and Sheehan, *The Iveragh Peninsula*, p. 135 (n = 190); Buckley and Sweetman, *Survey of county Louth*, p. 152 (n = 163). **22** Keegan, 'Ringforts in north Roscommon', p. 12; M. Scout, 'Ringforts', pp 207; Buckley and Sweetman, *Survey of county Louth*, p. 152.

Buckley believes that these sites were originally constructed without fosses, despite this being the easiest way of deriving the bank material.[23] Upon excavation, the full dimensions of a ringfort's defending fosse is often revealed. At Castle Balfour Demesne, Fermanagh, very slight surface evidence for a fosse between two banks was shown after excavation to have been 2m deep which would have been doubly impressive when viewed from the top of the inner bank.[24] At Raheennamadra, Limerick, a univallate ringfort had, prior to excavation, indications of an outer fosse only 0.60m deep but excavation showed it to be two and a half times deeper.[25]

Because the contemporary law tracts describe a king's principal dwelling to have been a univallate ringfort, some notion is obtained of the lofty status of bivallate, and extremely rare trivallate, sites. Multivallate sites, which tend not to have larger living areas than univallate examples, constitute *c*.19% of the ringfort population in many areas (see note 21). This is itself evidence for a consistent and widespread settlement hierarchy which must mirror a similar social stratification. Most bivallate ringforts have only one fosse. In the south west midlands, only one of the 37 bivallate sites have a second, or outer fosse,[26] while in Louth 78% of bivallate ringforts do not have a second fosse.[27] None of the four bivallate sites in north Roscommon have an outer fosse.[28] Perhaps a single intervening fosse is a diagnostic characteristic of most bivallate ringforts, in harmony with the law tracts which describe a double-banked ringfort with only one fosse. At Castle Balfour Demesne, attempts to locate the outer fosse of a bivallate ringfort produced 'no distinct, steep edges' in contrast to the steeply cut inner fosse.[29] Similarly, at Garryduff (I), the only fosse was excavated 2m into rock with almost all of the spoil being thrown inwards (creating a bank which still survives to a great height); and a small amount of spoil thrown outwards forming a slight outer bank.[30] Only one fosse was unearthed at the bivallate ringfort in Lisleagh (I).[31]

A ringfort's entrance usually consisted of an undug causeway across the fosse leading to a gap in the banks protected by a gate. G. Stout was the first to observe that the entrance was usually located in the east and south-east portion of the ringfort, regardless of the aspect of the land upon which the site was located.[32] 50% of entrances in the south-west midlands and 47% of entrances in north Kerry were orientated towards the east and south-east; in Cruachain 72% of sites with

23 Ibid., p. 152.   **24** N. Brannon, 'A rescue excavation at Lisdoo fort, Lisnaskea, county Fermanagh' in *Ulster Journal of Archaeology*, xliv–v (1981–2), pp 53–9, see p. 54.   **25** M. Stenberger, 'A ring-fort at Raheennamadra, Knocklong, Co. Limerick' in *Proceedings of the Royal Irish Academy*, lxv (1966), C, pp 37–54; see p. 39.   **26** M. Stout, 'Ringforts', p. 207.   **27** Buckley and Sweetman, *Survey of county Louth*, p. 152.   **28** Keegan, 'Ringforts in north Roscommon', p. 12.   **29** Brannon, 'Lisdoo fort', p. 55   **30** M. O'Kelly, 'Two ring-forts at Garryduff, Co. Cork' in *Proceedings of the Royal Irish Academy*, lxiii (1963), C, pp 17–125; see pp 18–22, pl. II.   **31** M. Monk, 'A tale of two ringforts: Lisleagh I and II' in *Journal of the Cork Historical and Archaeological Society*, c (1995), pp 105–16, sec p. 107.   **32** G. Stout, *lkerrin*, p. 29, fig. 20.).

identifiable entrances had eastern or southern orientations while 78% of ringforts had this orientation on the Iveragh Peninsula in Kerry. Two-third of ringforts in Louth, 55% of ringforts in parts of Leitrim, 46% in Donegal and 57% in Small County barony, Limerick, had entrances orientated between north-east and south-east.[33] The south-eastern positioning of entrances provided protection from the prevailing Irish (south-westerly) winds and colder winds from the north, as well as taking optimum advantage of available sunlight. The orientation of ringfort entrances accentuated the difference of status between two neighbouring ringforts at Lisleagh, Cork. The larger, bivallate ringfort (I) had an entrance orientated towards the south south-east, but 70m away the smaller, univallate site (II) had an exposed entrance in the west, facing towards the larger ringfort.[34]

A ringfort's overall diameter is a measure of both the size of its interior and the size and strength of its defences: 37% of ringforts in the south-west mid lands have overall diameters between 40m and 49m; 83% are between 30m and 60m.[35] Ó Ríordáin, Herity and Farrelly have noted that, in the more impressive ringforts, the actual living space often forms less than 60% of the total area of the monument.[36] Increasing a site's defences without a corresponding increase in its functional area demonstrates either a greater need for defence or an effort to display the status of the occupant.[37]

Some writers see the term 'ringfort' as a misnomer, for although ringforts were unquestionably fortified places, their defences had little martial significance.[38] Proudfoot goes so far as to suggest that the surrounding bank and ditch were 'little more than a fence to prevent stock from straying and a protection against wild animals'.[39] Mallory and McNeill argue that ringfort defences were defective in five key ways and that they were, therefore, merely constructed as a means of displaying social position: entrances across causeways were inherently weak; this weakness was accentuated by the absence of palisade enclosures along the top of the bank (if the negative evidence from many excavations is to be believed); fosses appear to have been allowed to silt up from the time of their construction; bivallate sites sometimes have their inner defences overlooked by the outer bank making it impossible, in those cases, to fall back from an outer position to an inner (this observation is not quantified in Mallory and McNeill's analysis and in the experience of this writer does not hold true: in north Roscommon, the outer banks of all four bivallate ringforts were less substantial than the inner rampart);[40] finally

33 M. Stout, 'Ringforts', p. 209, fig. 4c; Toal, *North Kerry*, p. 82; Herity, 'Cruachain III', pp 132–3, fig. 30a; O'Sullivan and Sheehan, The Iveragh Peninsula, p. 135; Buckley and Sweetman, *Survey of county Louth*, p. 152; Farrelly, 'Sample study', pp 36–7, fig. 18; G. Stout, *Ikerrin*, p. 30, fig. 21.   **34** Monk, 'Lisleagh I and II', pp 109–10.   **35** M. Stout, 'Ringforts', p. 209, fig. 4b   **36** Ó Ríordáin, *Antiquities*, p. 30; Herity, 'Cruachain III', pp 131–2, fig. 29c; Farrelly, 'Sample study', pp 27–34, figs 13–15.   **37** R. Warner, 'The archaeology of early historic Irish kingship', in S. Driscoll and M. Nieke (eds), *Power and politics in early medieval Britain and Ireland* (Edinburgh, 1988), pp 47–68; M. Stout, 'Ringforts', p. 217.   **38** Ó Ríordáin, *Antiquities*, p. 29.   **39** V. Proudfoot, 'The economy of the Irish rath' in *Medieval Archaeology*, v (1961), pp 94–122, see p. 94.   **40** Keegan, 'Ringforts in north Roscommon', p. 12.

Mallory and McNeill believe (perhaps without foundation) that a single family would have been unable to defend the 100m perimeter of a typical ringfort.[41] In the opinion of this writer, none of these deficiencies, other than the absence of a palisade, seriously challenges the defensive nature of ringforts and there is, in fact, evidence for a palisade from at least five ringfort excavations.[42] It is unlikely that a population which worked on a daily basis with post and wattle fencing and housing would not have erected a similar structure along the tops of at least some of their enclosures. Mallory and McNeill also fail to see ringforts in the context of their nearest neighbours. Mitchell has described how ringforts, although a form of dispersed settlement, were distributed in close enough proximity to one another to allow for neighbours to come rapidly to the aid of the occupants of endangered ringforts or, alternatively, to provide a place where fleeing victims could find shelter and regroup for counterattack. This strategy is best described as defence in depth.[43] The view from each ringfort in the Braid Valley in Antrim has been mapped by Black (fig. 1). It shows considerable overlapping of 'visual territories': even though most ringforts had no 'panoramic view' or 'extensive views' in only one direction, the location of ringforts was such that the occupants of one ringfort would have been in visual contact with as many as seventeen of their neighbours.[44]

Ringforts were not built to repel prolonged sieges designed to annex territories and populations, but rather to repel the lightning cattle raids which were endemic during the Early Christian period in Ireland.[45] It has been suggested also that ringforts could not have played a major defensive role in the days prior to artillery,[46] but this view does not consider the attitude of potential attackers to the ringfort occupants rather than to the ringforts themselves. The very knowledge that a ringfort contained a prominent, well-defended and well-connected individual must have acted as its own deterrent. In this way, the Early Christian mental landscape was well defended but in a manner which is less apparent to field workers today. Ultimately, the best testimony for the success of the ringfort as a settlement form is that so many of them were built. The size and complexity of enclosing banks tell us a great deal about the relative status of the ringfort occupants, but this fact should not obscure the primary defensive role of these enclosures which clearly met the day-to-day security needs of the farming families enclosed within them.

41 J. Mallory and T. McNeill, *The archaeology of Ulster* (Belfast, 1991), see pp 196–9.   42 O. Davies, 'Excavations at Lissachiggel' in *County Louth Archaeological Journal*, ix (1937–40), pp 209–43, see p. 214; Lynn, 'Rathmullan', appendix 6, p. 168 (Gransha); Edwards, *Early Medieval Ireland*, p. 20 (Killyliss); M. O'Kelly, 'Knockea, county Limerick' in E. Rynne (ed.), *North Munster studies: essays in commemoration of Monsignor Michael Moloney* (Limerick, 1967), pp 72–101, see pp 89–91; Monk, 'Lisleagh I and II', p. 107.   43 F. Mitchell, *Shell guide to reading the Irish landscape* (Dublin, 1986), see p. 156.   44 Black, 'The Braid and Upper Glenarm valleys', pp 14–15, fig. 11.   45 A. Lucas, *Cattle in ancient Ireland* (Kilkenny, 1989), see pp 125–99.   46 Seamus Caulfield, pers. comm.

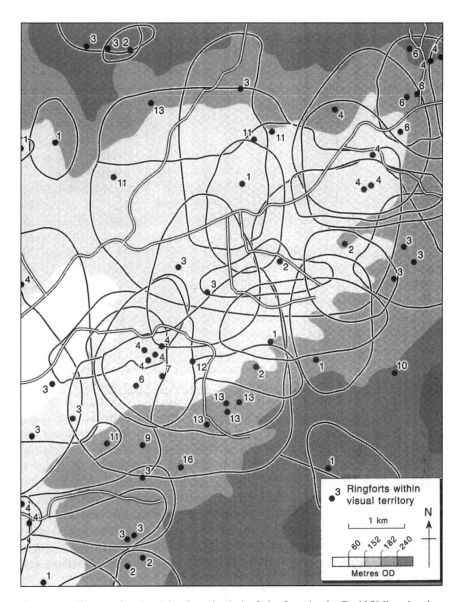

Figure 1   The overlapping 'visual territories' of ringforts in the Braid Valley, Antrim. Although ringforts are a form of dispersed settlement, their intervisibility afforded security beyond that provided by defensive banks and ditches (after Black, 1994).

2 Chronology

The dating of ringforts has caused controversy in the past and uncertainty about the time span of their occupation has retarded efforts to analyse their distribution as an indicator of the nature of Early Christian settlement and society. The sheer number of sites contrasts with the virtual absence of secular settlement for all prehistoric and historic periods prior to the seventeenth century. Because of their large number, it seemed logical to suggest that some ringforts might fill the void of settlement sites common in other periods.

Archaeological excavation, relying solely on stratigraphy as a dating devise, seemed at first to support this approach. Ó Ríordáin argued that a ringfort at Cush and its associated souterrain pre-dated a bronze age burial: the burial was stratified over a 'reddish layer of sand and clay' and this same sand and clay 'partly filled... and covered' the souterrain nearly 3m away. In retrospect, it is more probable that the souterrain was later than the burial and was in fact cut through and then backfilled with the layer in question.[1] A ringfort near the Turoe Stone in Galway was given a prehistoric date based on the discovery of a cist twenty years previous to the scientific excavation which produced finds consistent with Early Christian occupation in an area of considerable Iron Age activity.[2] Similarly, no convincing evidence has been presented to firmly fix another half dozen possibly early sites into the pre-Christian Iron Age.[3] At the other end of the time spectrum is the archaeologically unsustainable argument that many ringforts are medieval in date.[4] Rynne postulates a post-medieval date for a double-banked ringfort near Shannon Airport, concluding that a seventeenth-century rectangular house was contemporary with the construction of the enclosing banks.[5] He based his

1 S. Ó Ríordáin, 'Excavations at Cush, Co. Limerick' in *Proceedings of the Royal Irish Academy*, xlv (1940), C, pp 83–181, see pp 113, 177; Proudfoot, 'Economy', seep. 99. 2 J. Raftery, 'The Turoe Stone and the Rath of Feerwore' in *Journal of the Royal Society of Antiquaries of Ireland*, lxxiv (1944), pp 23–52; C. Lynn, 'Some 'early' ring-forts and crannógs' in *Journal of Irish Archaeology*, i (1983), pp 47–58, see p. 50. 3 S. Caulfield, 'Some Celtic problems in the Irish Iron Age' in Ó Corráin (ed.) *Irish Antiquity; essays and studies presented to Professor M. O'Kelly* (Cork, 1981), pp 205–15. 4 G. Barrett and B. Graham, 'Some consideration concerning the dating and distribution of ringforts in Ireland' in *Ulster Journal of Archaeology*, xxxix (1975), pp 33–45; C. Lynn, 'The dating of raths: an orthodox view' in *Ulster Journal of Archaeology*, xxxix (1975), pp 45–7. 5 E. Rynne, 'Ringforts at Shannon Airport' in *Proceedings of the Royal Irish Academy*, lxiii (1964), C, pp 245–77.

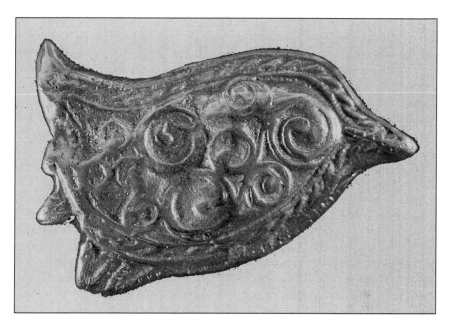

Plate 1   The 'Garryduff bird'; a seventh-century gold ornament found in a bivallate ringfort in Cork (Cork Museum)

conclusions solely on stratigraphic evidence, which can be problematic, especially in the case of structures set into wall foundations dug through earlier layers. Overall, the stratigraphical approach to dating ringforts has proved unsatisfactory on many excavations.

Despite the extremes in date produced from a few excavations, it is still widely accepted that most ringforts date from the Early Christian period. Finds from ringforts typically include items which date from the second half of the first millennium: wheel-made pottery, especially E ware;[6] a coarse pottery indigenous to Ireland known as souterrain ware;[7] glass beads; bone, bronze and iron pins; and artefacts of bone and metalwork dated to the period on art-historical grounds. The Garryduff bird is one of the most spectacular examples of a dateable find from a ringfort (plate 1): this small (16mm) but beautifully decorated gold ornament was made *c*.AD650 and dropped during or soon after the construction of an impressive bivallate ringfort.[8]

---

6 C. Thomas, 'Imported pottery in Dark-Age western Britain' in *Medieval Archaeology*, iii (1959), pp 89–111.   7 M. Ryan, 'Native pottery in early historic Ireland' in *Proceedings of the Royal Irish Academy*, lxxiii (1973), C, pp 619–45.   8 O'Kelly, 'Garryduff', fig. 1, pp 119–20, pl. VIII.

This more common and widely accepted dating evidence is confirmed using the modern technique of dendrochronology and the increasingly refined use of radiocarbon dating. Oak samples from excavations can be dated to within a year. In turn, the dendrochronological records provide a basis on which to calibrate radiocarbon results and thus to enhance this method.[9] Modern dating methods suggest a much shorter span of years for the construction and occupation of ringforts and allied crannóg lake settlements than was indicated by the earlier, less certain stratigraphical evidence. The best known of the precisely dated sites is the platform ringfort at Deer Park Farms, Antrim. Due to the waterlogged conditions there, the door-jambs of a house from the primary occupation phase still survived and one of these was made from an oak tree felled in AD648.[10]

Figure 2 and table 1 present the scientific dating evidence from 47 sites. A total of 114 dendro and calibrated radiocarbon dates span the years AD236 (probably from a pre-ringfort occupation phase) to AD1387; over half of the determinations (54%) fall within AD540 and AD884 while nearly two-thirds of sites have the mid-point of their date range falling between AD600 and AD900. A careful re-examination of the excavations of both early and late dated sites listed in table 1 would, no doubt, narrow the range still further. Although 64% of the dated sites are in Ulster (one-third are from Antrim alone), there is no suggestion of any regional variation in the range of dates. However, these dates do highlight how archaeological research into the Early Christian period has been dominated by Ulster archaeologists. The firm conclusion is that the majority of Ireland's ringforts and crann6gs were occupied and probably con structed during a three-hundred-year period from the beginning of the seventh-century to the end of the ninth-century AD.

Table 1: Scientifically dated ringforts and associated site[11]
(Figures in italics are tree-ring dates)

No.	Location	Site type	Date		Lab-no.
		CONNAUGHT			
1	Ballybeg 6, Sligo[12]	Cashel	693	884	LU-1758
2	Carrowmore 2, Sligo[13]	Cashel	434	635	LU-1752
3	Cloverhill Lough, Sligo[14]	Crannóg ·	883	1024	ST-7622
4	Cloverhill Lough, Sligo	Crannóg	886	992	LU-1841
5	Culeenamore 15, Sligo[15]	Kitchen midden	689	980	FRA-53

9 M. Baillie, 'Dating the past' in M. Ryan (ed.), *The illustrated archaeology of Ireland* (Dublin 1991), pp 15–19.   10 Lynn, 'Deer Park Farms', pp 11–15.   11 Dates in calibrated years AD and are given within plus or minus one standard deviation.   12 G. Burenhult, *The archaeology of Carrowmore: environmental archaeology and the megalithic tradition at Carrowmore, county Sligo, Ireland* (Stockholm, 1984), pp 71, 132.   13 Ibid., p. 132.   14 Ibid., p. 126.   15 Ibid., pp 132, 338, 345.

No.	Location	Site type	Date		Lab-no.
6	Grange West 1, Sligo[16]	Cashel	781	981	LU-1753
7	Grange West 1, Sligo	Cashel	993	1148	LU-1754
8	Grange West 2, Sligo[17]	Ringfort	544	798	ST-7623
9	Grange West 2, Sligo	Ringfort	651	777	LU-1838
10	Lufferton 8, Sligo[18]	Cashel	689	865	LU-1756
11	Seafield 11, Sligo[19]	Cashel	660	776	LU-1757

LEINSTER

No.	Location	Site type	Date		Lab-no.
12	Dunbell, Kilkenny[20]	Ringfort	584	659	UB-3389
13	Dunbell, Kilkenny	Ringfort	655	798	UB-3410
14	Dunbell, Kilkenny	Ringfort	664	768	UB-3392
15	Dunbell, Kilkenny	Ringfort	694	876	UB-3391
16	Dunbell, Kilkenny	Ringfort	779	940	UB-3390
17	Dunbell, Kilkenny	Ringfort	882	981	UB-3412
18	Aghadegnan, Longford[21]	Ringfort	408	543	UB-3461
19	Aghadegnan, Longford	Ringfort	428	597	UB-3459
20	Aghadegnan, Longford	Ringfort	431	577	UB-3454
21	Aghadegnan, Longford	Ringfort	560	640	UB-3455
22	Aghadegnan, Longford	Ringfort	607	656	UB-3451
23	Aghadegnan, Longford	Ringfort	687	776	UB-3456
24	Aghadegnan, Longford	Ringfort	690	795	UB-3458
25	Aghadegnan, Longford	Ringfort	900	1019	UB-3452
26	Marshes Upper, Louth[22]	Ringfort	663	797	UB-2572
27	Marshes Upper, Louth	Ringfort	783	983	UB-2573
28	*Moynagh Lough, Meath[23]*	*Crannóg*	*625*	*625*	*QUB*
29	*Moynagh Lough, Meath*	*Crannóg*	*748*	*748*	*QUB*

MUNSTER

No.	Location	Site type	Date		Lab-no.
30	Conva, Cork[24]	Ringfort	434	602	UB-3638
31	Conva, Cork	Ringfort	642	685	UB-3635
32	Killanully, Cork[25]	Ringfort	775	880	UB-3647
33	Killanully, Cork	Souterrain	783	980	UB-3649
34	Killanully, Cork	Ringfort	991	1208	UB-3648

---

16 Ibid., p. 72.   **17** Ibid., pp 73, 80, 91.   **18** Ibid., p. 98.   **19** Ibid., pp 71, 132.   **20** My thanks to Beth Cassidy, ADS Ltd, for granting permission to use these dates in advance of publication.   **21** My thanks to Judith Carroll for granting permission to use these dates in advance of publication.   **22** Gowan, 'Excavations of two souterrain complexes at Marshes Upper, Dundalk, county Louth' in *Proceedings of the Royal Irish Academy*, xcii (1992), C, 55–121.   **23** J. Bradley, 'Excavations at Moynagh Lough, county Meath' in *Journal of the Royal Society of Antiquaries of Ireland*, cxxi (1991), pp 5–26; this was a reused timber, see pp 15–18.   **24** M. Doody, 'Ballyhoura Hills project; Interim report' in *Discovery Programme reports: 1; Project results 1992*, (Dublin 1993), pp 20–30.   **25** C. Mount, 'Excavations at Killanully, county Cork' in *Proceedings of the Royal Irish Academy*, xcv, C (1995), pp 119–57, see p. 156.

No.	*Location*	*Site type*	*Date*		*Lab-no.*
35	Lisleagh (1), Cork[26]	Ringfort	608	688	UB-2688
36	Lisleagh (1), Cork	Ringfort	659	776	UB-2608
37	Lisleagh (1), Cork[27]	Ringfort	662	770	UB-2548
38	Lisleagh (1), Cork	Ringfort	662	867	UB-2549
49	Lisleagh (1), Cork[28]	Ringfort	776	989	UB-2689
40	Lisleagh (1), Cork[29]	Ringfort	902	1145	UB-2607
41	Lisnagun, Cork[30]	Souterrain	894	991	UB-3178
42	Lisnagun, Cork	Ringfort	1031	1215	UB-3177
43	Ballingarry Down, Limerick[31]	Ringfort	643	882	
44	Raheennamadra, Limerick[32]	Ringfort	606	775	Uppsala
45	Raheennamadra, Limerick	Ringfort	643	882	Uppsala
46	Raheennamadra, Limerick[33]	Souterrain	649	938	Uppsala
47	Raheennamadra, Limerick	Souterrain	655	975	Uppsala

ULSTER

48	Antiville, Antrim[34]	Ringfort	544	644	UB?
49	Antiville, Antrim[35]	Ringfort	695	936	UB?
50	Ballyhenry, Antrim[36]	Ringfort	649	690	UB-945
51	Ballyhenry, Antrim	Ringfort	983	1020	UB-946
52	Ballynoe, Antrim[37]	Earthwork	641	777	UB-908
53	Ballyutoag, Antrim[38]	Ringfort	654	879	UB-2637
54	Ballyutoag, Antrim[39]	Ringfort	690	939	UB-2596
55	Deer Park Farms, Antrim[40]	Ringfort	608	663	UB-3217

26 My thanks to Michael Monk for granting permission to use these dates in advance of publication.   **27** Lynn, 'Houses', ii, p. 51, structure 3.   **28** My thanks to Michael Monk for granting permission to use these dates in advance of publication.   **29** Lynn, 'Houses', p. 51, structure 3.   **30** Jerry O'Sullivan, pers. comm. The sample from an abandoned souterrain was thought to be later than the sample which produced the twelfth-century date. The excavator believes, therefore, that it is possible that both dates are unacceptable due to contamination of the samples or mistakes made in the recording of the samples during excavation. My thanks to Jerry O'Sullivan for granting permission to use these dates in advance of publication.   **31** O'Flaherty, Locational analysis of the ringfort, p. 26.   **32** M. Stenberger, 'A ring-fort at Raheennamadra, Knocklong, county Limerick' in *Proceedings of the Royal Irish Academy*, lxv C (1966), pp 37–54; from hearth, p. 52.   **33** Stenberger, 'Raheennamadra', p. 52; from oak posts of souterrain within ringfort.   **34** C. Lynn, 'Houses', ii, p. 4.   **35** Lynn, 'Houses', ii, p. 4; date from The Queen's University of Belfast derived from same sample that produced a date of AD480 from Trinity College Dublin.   **36** C. Lynn, 'Two raths at Ballyhenry, county Antrim' in *Ulster Journal of Archaeology*, xlvi (1983), pp 67–91.   **37** C. Lynn, 'The excavation of an earthwork enclosure at Ballynoe, county Antrim' in *Ulster Journal of Archaeology*, xliii (1980), pp 29–38. This sub-rectangular Early Christian habitation site does not appear to be a ringfort in the usual sense.   **38** B. Williams, 'Excavations at Ballyutoag, county Antrim' in *Ulster journal of Archaeology*, xlvii (1984), pp 37–49; phase 2.   **39** Ibid., phase 4.   **40** My thanks to Chris Lynn and the Environment and Heritage Service, Department of Environment (NI) for granting permission to use these dates in advance of publication.

No.	Location	Site type	Date		Lab-no.
56	*Deer Park Farms, Antrim[41]*	*Ringfort*	*648*	*648*	*QUB*
57	Deer Park Farms, Antrim[42]	Ringfort	669	766	UB-3084
58	Deer Park Farms, Antrim	Ringfort	672	766	UB-3081
59	Deer Park Farms, Antrim	Ringfort	687	771	UB-3064
60	Deer Park Farms, Antrim	Ringfort	688	773	UB-3082
61	Deer Park Farms, Antrim	Ringfort	689	776	UB-3083
62	Deer Park Farms, Antrim	Ringfort	691	777	UB-3093
63	Deer Park Farms, Antrim	Ringfort	693	797	UB-3200
64	Deer Park Farms, Antrim	Ringfort	694	801	UB-3065
65	Deer Park Farms, Antrim	Ringfort	776	865	UB-3066
66	Deer Park Farms, Antrim	Ringfort	782	940	UB-3199
67	Deer Park Farms, Antrim	Ringfort	784	943	UB-3201
68	Dunsilly, Antrim[43]	Ringfort	408	637	UB-2001
69	Dunsilly, Antrim[44]	Ringfort	1065	1214	UB-890
70	Killealy, Antrim[45]	Ringfort	359	537	UB-536
71	Killealy, Antrim	Ringfort	409	542	UB-538
72	Killealy, Antrim	Ringfort	428	615	UB-539
73	Killealy, Antrim	Ringfort	429	556	UB-541
74	Killealy, Antrim	Ringfort	544	644	UB-537
75	Killealy, Antrim[46]	Ringfort	614	668	UB-546
76	Killealy, Antrim	Ringfort	642	686	UB-540
77	Killealy, Antrim	Ringfort	645	769	UB-542
78	Killealy, Antrim[47]	Ringfort	693	881	UB-544
79	*Kilnock, Antrim[48]*	*Crannóg*	*713*	*731*	*QUB*
80	*Lough Tamin, Antrim*	*Crannóg*	*609*	*627*	*QUB*
81	*Midges Island, Antrim*	*Crannóg*	*561*	*579*	*QUB*
82	Poleglass, Antrim[49]	Ringfort	624	975	UB-921
83	Poleglass, Antrim	Ringfort	898	1025	UB-920
84	Seacash, Antrim[50]	Ringfort	562	664	UB-671
85	Seacash, Antrim	Ringfort	777	981	UB-672
86	Seacash, Antrim	Ringfort	1216	1282	UB-673

41 Lynn, 'Deer Park Farms'. **42** My thanks to Chris Lynn and the Environment and Heritage Service, Department of Environment (NI) for granting permission to use these dates in advance of publication. **43** C. Lynn, 'The excavation of Rathmullan, a raised rath and motte in county Down' in *Ulster journal of Archaeology*, xliv-v (1981–2), pp 65–171, app. 6, p. 168, last pre-ring fort phase. **44** Ibid., phase three. **45** Ibid. **46** Ibid, second occupation. **47** Ibid., build-up phase of raised ringfort. **48** M. Baillie, 'An interim statement on dendrochronology at Belfast' in *Ulster journal of Archaeology*, xiii (1979), pp 72–84. **49** Radio-carbon laboratory, Palaeoecology Centre, The Queen's University of Belfast. **50** C. Lynn, 'A rath in Seacash townland, county Antrim' in *Ulster Journal of Archaeology*, xii (1978), pp 55–74.

No.	Location	Site type	Date		Lab–no.
87	Teeshan, Antrim[51]	Crannóg	581	581	QUB
88	Teeshan, Antrim	Crannóg	444	462	QUB
89	Tully, Antrim[52]	Ringfort	610	689	UB?
90	Tully, Antrim	Ringfort	645	769	UB?
91	Big Glebe, Derry[53]	Ringfort	686	777	UB-2153
92	Big Glebe, Derry	Ringfort	882	986	UB-2152
93	Big Glebe, Derry	Ringfort	1026	1156	UB-2151
94	Crossnacreevy, Down[54]	Ringfort	653	690	UB-674
95	Drumaroad, Down[55]	Ringfort	886	1153	?
96	Rathmullan Lower, Down[56]	Ringfort	540	637	UB-2526
97	Rathmullan Lower, Down[57]	Ringfort	885	985	UB-2527
98	Rathmullan Lower, Down[58]	Ringfort	902	996	UB-2525
99	Castle Balfour, Fermanagh[59]	Ringfort	359	428	UB-2202
100	Coolcran, Fermanagh[60]	Souterrain	813	831	QUB
101	Killfoal Lough, Fermanagh[61]	Crannóg	544	562	QUB
102	Ross Lough, Fermanagh	Crannóg	561	579	QUB
103	Island McHugh, Tyrone	Crannóg	613	631	QUB
104	Killyliss, Tyrone[62]	Ringfort	778	978	UB-2620
105	Killyliss, Tyrone	Ringfort	1279	1387	UB-2622
106	Killyliss, Tyrone	Ringfort	643	766	UB-2621
107	Killyliss, Tyrone	Ringfort	783	985	UB-2623
108	Lisdoo, Tyrone	Ringfort	359	428	UB-2202
109	Mullaghbane, Tyrone[63]	Ringfort	236	427	UB-390
110	Mullaghbane, Tyrone	Ringfort	1155	1283	UB?
111	Burghead?[64]	Ringfort	899	1016	UB-2083
112	Catherwoods?	Ringfort	605	687	UB-663
113	Derrymowlaght?	Crannóg	690	856	UB-3719
114	Lismunshin?	Crannóg	243	341	UB-3383

51 Baillie, 'An interim statement'.   **52** *Radiocarbon*, xv (1973), pp 215–16.   **53** Lynn, 'Rathmullan'. See app. 6, p. 168; three dates from one house.   **54** A. Harper, 'The excavation of a rath in Crossnacreevy townland, county Down', in *Ulster Journal of Archaeology*, xxxvi–vii (1974–4), pp 32–41. This report contains a description of the local Early Christian environment.   **55** D. Waterman, 'The excavation of a house and souterrain at Whitefort, Drumarood, county Down' in *Ulster Journal of Archaeology*, xix (1956), 73–86.   **56** C. Lynn, 'The excavation of Rathmullan, county Down: Addenda' in *Ulster Journal of Archaeology*, xlviii (1985), pp 130–1.   **57** Ibid., construction phase.   **58** Ibid., destruction phase.   **59** N. Brannon, 'A rescue excavation at Lisdoo Fort, Lisnaskea, county Fermanagh' in *Ulster Journal of Archaeology*, xliv–v (1981–2), pp 53–9. From a pre-ringfort phase, see fig. 2, trench 7, layer 6.   **60** B. Williams, 'Excavation of a rath at Coolcran, county Fermanagh' in *Ulster Journal of Archaeology*, xlviii (1985), pp 69–79. Date from wooden souterrain contemporary with ringfort.   **61** Baillie, 'An interim statement'.   **62** R. Ivens, 'Killyliss rath, county Tyrone' in *Ulster Journal of Archaeology*, xlvii (1984), pp 9–35.   **63** Lynn, 'Houses', p. ii, p. 137.   **64** Radio-carbon laboratory, Palaeoecology Centre, The Queen's University of Belfast.

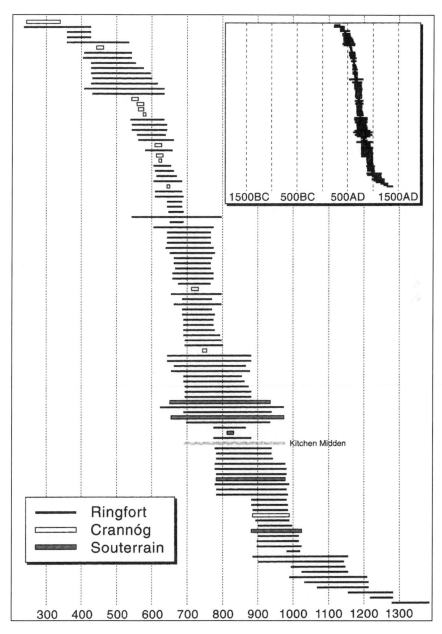

1500BC   500BC   500AD   1500AD

Kitchen Midden

—— Ringfort
☐ Crannóg
▣ Souterrain

300 400 500 600 700 800 900 1000 1100 1200 1300

Figure 2   Radiocarbon and dendrochronological dating evidence for ringforts and associated sites. These dates points toward a period between AD600 and AD900 for the construction of most ringforts. Although it has been suggested that ringforts were occupied from the Bronze Age (*c.*1800 BC) to the PostMedieval period (*c.*1700), the inset emphasises their Early Christian date.

Further, the dating of different phases of occupation in some ringforts shows two-thirds of them to have been in use over a period spanning at least two centuries. Lynn's summary of the excavations of platform ringforts lists those sites which had more than one phase of occupation: Rathmullan, Down (4 ringfort phases); Sallagh Fort, Antrim (2 phases); Ballynarry, Down (3 phases); Carnmoney, Antrim (2 phases); and Dunsilly, Antrim (3 phases between c.AD385 and c.AD1060).[65] Deer Park Farms had six distinct construction phases[66] and the stratigraphy was so complex at the water-logged site of Ballingarry Down, Limerick that the excavation was abandoned.[67] Two phases of use were revealed in an aerial photograph of the levelled remains of a large ringfort at Newtown, north Dublin. Originally a bivallate ringfort with an internal diameter of 45m, this site was later enlarged into a trivallate site with an internal diameter of 75m.[68] Barrett cites seven further ringforts whose thick habitation layers and complex structural history indicate occupation over a considerable period: Croft Road, Holywood, Down; Oldcourt, Cork; Knockea, Limerick; Duneight, Down; Langford Lodge, Antrim; Dressogagh, Armagh; and Beal Boru, Clare.[69]

The platform ringfort of Rathmullan was occupied continuously in four major phases between the eighth and twelfth centuries at which point it was converted into a motte. At first sight this seems to be evidence for the continued occupation of ringforts into the period immediately preceding the coming of the Normans. Yet the initial phase, which spanned the sixth to eight centuries, had a markedly different economic basis – cattle and sheep were of primary importance – to the later phases when a tillage-based economy seems to have developed.[70] Thus, even where spatial continuity is evident, economic and functional continuity can be questionable.

If the majority of ringforts were built during a period of three centuries, and if many ringforts were multi-phase sites, as the above stratigraphical and dating

---

65 Lynn, 'Rathmullan', appendix 6, p. 168.   **66** C. Lynn, 'Deer Park Farms' in C. Cotter (ed.), *Excavations 1985* (Dublin, 1986), pp 9–10.   **67** Frank Mitchell pers. comm.; see also Lynn, 'Rathmullan', appendix 6, p. 166   **68** G. Stout and M. Stout, 'Patterns in the past: county Dublin 5000 BC–1000 AD' in F. Aalen and K. Whelan (eds), *Dublin: from prehistory to present: Studies in honour of J.H. Andrews* (Dublin, 1992), pp 5–25, see p. 18, fig. 5.   **69** V. Proudfoot, 'Note on a rath at Croft Road, Holywood, county Down' in *Ulster Journal of Archaeology*, xxii (1959), pp 102–6; C. Ó Cuileanáin and T. Murphy, 'A ringfort at Oldcourt, county Cork' in *Journal of the Cork Historical and Archaeological Society*, lxvi (1961), pp 79–92; O'Kelly, 'Knockea', pp 72–101; D. Waterman, 'Excavations at Duneight, county Down' in *Ulster Journal of Archaeology*, xxvi (1963), pp 55–78 (ref. to Langford Lodge); A. Collins, 'Excavations at Dressogagh rath' in *Ulster Journal of Archaeology*, xxix (1966), pp 117–29, see pp 126–29; M. O'Kelly, 'Beal Boru, county Clare' in *Journal of the Cork Historical and Archaeological Society*, lxvii (1962), pp 1–27, see pp 12–15.   **70** F. McCormick, 'Farming and food in medieval Lecale' in L. Proudfoot (ed.), *Down; history and society Down: interdisciplinary essays on the history of an Irish county* (Dublin, 1997), pp 33–46, see table 1.

evidence suggests, then it becomes more likely that many ringforts are contemporary with one another. The excavations at Lisleagh, Cork, have confirmed that while the construction of one ringfort probably preceded another, two neighbouring sites existed simultaneously.[71] The analysis of distribution based on surviving settlement evidence was a questionable pursuit when it was felt that these sites spanned a 1,500 year period of construction; however, current evidence makes it tenable to assume site contemporaneity, an assumption implicit in most models of Early Christian settlement and the underlying assumption of this study.

71 Monk, 'Lisleagh I and II', p. 113.

3 Function

From their dispersed distribution and the predominantly rural nature of Early Christian society, it is accepted that ringforts represent the Irish version of a common European settlement pattern known as *einzelhofe* – or dispersed individual farmsteads. This term comes from Meitzen's early work which suggested a Celtic or 'Germanic' origin for this settlement pattern.[1] Most excavated ringforts have revealed the foundations of a range of buildings within their banks indicating that the surviving monuments were in fact farmsteads which would have enclosed a single farming family and their retainers. Some internal structures were large enough to be houses while others could only have functioned as sheds or byres. Cashels often have traces of stone-built house foundations within them. Lynn has made these houses the focus of his research and his conclusions have a bearing on the function, dating and population housed within ringforts.[2] Approximately 250 small domestic and ancillary structures associated with ringforts have been recorded by Lynn from the Early Christian period. It has been possible to identify 137 of these as houses: 77 were circular in plan and 60 rectangular.[3] In 14 out of 16 cases where there was evidence for a sequence of house types at one site, it was usual for rectangular houses to have replaced circular ones.[4] Lynn concludes that rectangular buildings were introduced and used at a time when many of the enclosures in which they were built were falling out of use; thus the houses indicate social and economic continuity but not a specific desire to continue living within ringforts. This accounts for the fact that 19 of 20 houses found outside but adjacent to ringforts were rectangular and that rectangular houses within ringforts were most commonly located near the bank, a vulnerable location considering a ringfort's primary defensive function. Because of the differing shapes (rectangular house against curvilinear bank), it could be said that the use of rectangular buildings in ringforts was incongruous, perhaps culturally unstable, and that it almost certainly dated to the end of the period during which ringforts were in use.[5] Also associated with this late, post-ringfort settlement phase were souterrains which were generally entered from rectangular houses. The

1 A. Meitzen, *Siedelung und agratwesen der Westgem,anen und Ostermanen der Kelten, Romer, Finnen und Slawen* (Berlin, 1895), see vol. iii, pp 174–82. My thanks to Martin Reinicke for his translation of this source.   2 Lynn, Houses.   3 Ibid., i, p. 145, table 12:1.   4 Ibid., i, p. 163.   5 Ibid., i, p. 150.

construction and occupation of ringforts may have tapered off, according to this evidence, well before the coming of the Normans, with unfortified open settlement, often with rectangular houses and perhaps souterrains being preferred from *c*.AD1000.[6] This change in settlement pattern was, in Doherty's view, accompanied by and perhaps attributable to the demise of the tuath structure which was replaced by a more 'modern' feudal system of administration.[7]

Circular houses, which are directly associated with the main phase of ringfort occupation, tend to be located towards the centre of the enclosure placing them furthest from an attack from outside the bank (59% – 27 out of 46 examples). House doors faced mainly to the east (71%), which meant that the view from most houses was towards the general direction of the ringfort entrance, whilst providing maximum protection from the prevailing winds.[8] Of the circular houses discussed by Lynn, 59 (77%) were between 3.5m and 7m in diameter. Definite sites (10 houses) had a modal diameter of 6m while most houses had an area of *c*.28.29m²,[9] which comparative ethnographic research suggests would have accommodated five or six persons.[10] The dimension, number and purpose of buildings found within ringforts is confirmed in contemporary legal sources (see below chapter 7).

It is possible that some ringforts functioned throughout their existence only as cattle enclosures, or as enclosed structures with no domestic function. A number of excavations have produced no evidence at all for occupation. Examples include: the partial excavations of Garryduff II, Cork; Lisdrumchor, Armagh; Tullyallan, Armagh; and Lisnavaragh, Down.[11] The lack of finds at Ballysillan, Antrim; Seafin, Down; and Lackan III, Wicklow is best explained by the limited extent of the excavations at these sites and disturbance on the site prior to excavation.[12] Since it seems unlikely that a ringfort once constructed was never used, it is possible that some of these sites functioned exclusively as livestock enclosures; but the possibility that the excavators failed to recognise human settlement evidence in the sampled

---

6 Ibid., i, p. v.   7 C. Doherty, pers. comm.   8 Ibid., i, pp 160, 147.   9 Ibid., i, pp 151–2.   10 Ibid., i, pp 136, 159. See also: K. Chang, 'Study of the Neolithic social grouping: examples from the New World', *American Anthropologist*, lx (1958), 298–334. In American Neolithic societies examined by Chang, the size of the house correlated with the size of the household except for occasional privileged persons; S. Casselberry, 'Further refinement of formulae for determining population from floor area' in *World Archaeology*, vi (1974), 118–22. According to Casselberry, a building of 6–7m would have accommodated 5 or 6 occupants.   11 Listed in Proudfoot, 'Economy of the Irish rath', p. 106, table 1 and Barrett, 'The ring-fort', p. 131. O'Kelly, 'Garryduff, pp 17–125; Association of Young Irish Archaeologists, *Excavations 1971* (Belfast, 1972), pp 7–8; E. Jope (ed.), *The archaeological survey of county Down* (Belfast, 1966), see p. 150.   12 Listed in Proudfoot, Economy of the Irish rath, p. 106, table 1 and Barrett, The ring-fort, p. 131; E. Evans, 'Excavations at Mount Royal and Ballysillan, county Antrim' in *Ulster Journal of Archaeology*, xv (1952), pp 84–6; D. Waterman, 'Excavations at Seafin castle and Ballyroney motte and bailey' in *Ulster Journal of Archaeology*, xviii (1955), pp 83–104; M. O'Connor, 'The excavation of three earthen ring-forts in the Liffey valley' in *Journal of the Royal Society of Antiquaries of Ireland*, lxxiv (1944), pp 53–60.

areas of rushed excavations cannot be entirely ruled out. Some tentative evidence exists to suggest that a ringfort could have a domestic function at first which would later become an enclosure exclusively for the safekeeping of animals. For example, a house within a ringfort in Lisnagade, Down is believed by the excavator to have been replaced by a three-sided barn.[13]

---

13 Proudfoot, 'Economy of the Irish rath', p. 95

4 Economy

The economy practised by the ringfort occupants has been summarised by Proudfoot based on excavations published between 1925 and 1955,[1] and subsequent research has not altered the broad strokes of his conclusions. Although the occupants of ringforts practised a mixed agriculture, finds and contemporary sources indicate that cattle rearing was their principal economic pursuit. More recently, McCormick has analysed faunal remains and deduced the minimum number of beasts represented from nine Early Christian settlement sites producing evidence for more than twenty individual animals. This confirms the importance of domesticated livestock, especially cattle, to the Early Christian economy. Cattle constituted between 19% and 71% of individual animals found at the various sites and 47% of 1,132 animals identified. Pigs represented between 8% and 57% of animals found at the nine sites and 30% of the total. Sheep represented between 9% and 51% of animals found at the individual sites, but only 23% of the total. Deer Park Farms, the most recent ringfort excavation examined by McCormick, produced a faunal record remarkably similar to the mean from the nine aforementioned Early Christian settlement sites: 47% cattle, 31% pigs, 22% sheep.[2] Similarly, cattle constituted 45% of livestock remains at Marshes Upper, Louth.[3] The minimum number of individuals obscures the key importance of cattle in the archaeological record because of their greater size and productivity. Cattle, in fact, only appear as food in the archaeological record as a by-product of dairy activity. Nonetheless, McCormick's analysis of the faunal remains from three important Early Christian excavations in Meath (Moynagh Lough and Lagore crannógs, and Knowth) revealed that the composition of the dairy herd (71% females to 29% males) exactly mirrored the dairy herd as described in *Críth Gablach*.[4] Sheep also had a function other than as a source for protein in that they were kept for their wool but this was not important within the context of the overall economy as there

---

1 V. Proudfoot, 'Economy of the Irish rath', p. 97.   2 F. McCormick, 'The effects of the Anglo-Norman settlement on Ireland's wild and domesticated fauna' in P. Crabtree and K. Ryan (eds), *Animal use and culture change*, MASCA research papers in science and archaeology, (supplement) viii (Philadelphia, 1991), pp 40–52, see pp 41–2, table 1.   3 Gowan, 'Two souterrain complexes at Marshes Upper', appendix I, table 1, p. 114.   4 F. McCormick, 'Dairying and beef production in Early Christian Ireland; the faunal evidence', in T. Reeves–Smyth and F. Hamond (eds), *Landscape archaeology* (Oxford, 1983), pp 253–67, see pp 256, 259.

were not any significant wool exports from Ireland for much of the Early Christian period.[5] A factor which further reduced the importance of sheep was their tendency to be smaller in Ireland than elsewhere in Europe, resulting in smaller quantities of wool and meat.[6] Pigs were reared exclusively for slaughter and it is possible that they were housed with humans within ringforts (as evidenced by pig-specific lice found in association with human head lice and fleas at Deer Park Farms).[7] This may explain how neo-natal pigs found their way into the souterrain at Marshes Upper, ringfort 3.[8] The platform ringfort at Rathmullan is unusual in having a large percentage (over 50%) of pig bones present which may indicate a more intensive tillage economy in the Ards peninsula, but even here, pig bones represented only 16% of the total during the original sixth- to eighth-century habitation phase.[9] The occupants of ringforts also called upon a wide range of foodstuffs to provide a degree of variety in a diet dominated by milk products: red deer, fish and shellfish remains are commonly found at ringfort excavations.[10]

The importance of cattle seems to have its origins in the prehistoric Iron Age. The *Táin*, perhaps incorporating oral tales which originated in that period, demonstrate this early pre-occupation with cattle. It is possible, however, that the significance of dairy cattle to the Irish economy was a later, Early Christian development.[11] It has long been held that the slaughter of calves at an early age, noted in excavated sites as far back as the Middle Bronze Age, is an indication of dairying, calves being in direct competition with the human population for milk. However, the saint's lives and laws draw attention to the need, in primitive breeds, for the calves to be present at milking in order for cows to release their milk. Accordingly, calves being slaughtered in the first nine months is evidence against dairying in primitive herds. McCormick believes that the trait of releasing milk only when calves were present would have been bred out of the cattle if dairying had begun over a thousand years earlier. A prehistoric date has been attributed to the introduction of dairying in Britain and Ireland on the basis of such evidence as at, for instance, the Middle Bronze Age site of Grimes Graves, Norfolk, where 45% of cattle were slaughtered before they were eight months (fig. 3). In contrast, only four percent of cattle from that age group were slaughtered at Moynagh Lough crann6g, Meath. The possibility that dairying, and the resulting improvement in diet, was introduced at the beginning of the Early Christian period could help to explain the upsurge in population which is implicit in the evidence for the widespread construction of settlement sites during such a brief period.

5 McCormick, 'Ireland's wild and domesticated fauna', p. 42.   6 Ibid., p. 42, table 2.   7 H. Kenward and E. Allison, 'A preliminary view of the insect assemblages from the Early Christian rath site at Deer Park Farms, Northern Ireland' in J. Rackham (ed.), *Environment and economy in Anglo-Saxon England* (York, 1994), pp 89–103, see p. 96.   8 Gowan, 'Two souterrain complexes; see F. McCormick in appendix I, p. 118.   9 McCormick, 'Ireland's wild and domesticated fauna', table 1.   10 Proudfoot, 'Economy of the Irish rath', pp 113–5.   11 F. McCormick, 'Early fauna! evidence for dairying' in *Oxford journal of Archaeology*, xi (1992), pp 201–9.

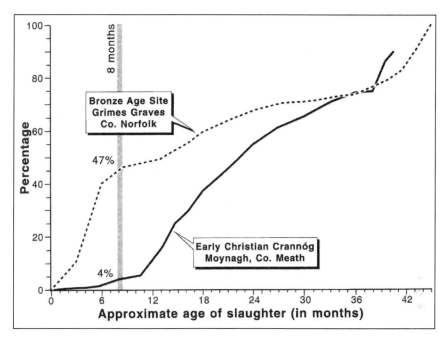

Figure 3 The slaughter of calves at an early age in the Middle Bronze Age site of Grimes Graves (where 45% of cattle were slaughtered before they were eight months old) does not indicate the presence of dairying in prehistoric Britain and Ireland. The pattern at Moynagh Lough (only four per cent of cattle from that age group were slaughtered) may be evidence for the introduction of dairying in the Late Iron Age/Early Christian period. At the introductory stage of dairying, cows would have required calves to be present to stimulate the lactation process (after McCormick, 1992).

As with livestock, most excavated ringforts provide some evidence for tillage and the small petal-shaped fields associated with ringforts may have been the location for this tillage activity. In the embryonic stages of enclosing the landscape, it is more likely that animals were fenced out rather than in. Corn drying kilns have been identified in four of the forty-six ringfort excavations examined by Proudfoot and eight sites have produced evidence for ploughs and other iron tools associated with tillage.[12] Twenty sites have produced quern stones, and while this shows how widespread the use of cereals in the diet of ringfort occupants was, it is also indicative of the low grinding capacity necessary to meet their needs. In contrast, horizontal water mills are most often found in association with ecclesiastical sites.[13] An exception to this, however, is the discovery of a wooden paddle from a horizontal mill in the water-logged conditions at Deer Park Farms ringfort. Similar evidence

12 Proudfoot, 'Economy of the Irish rath', table 1.   13 Swan, pers. Comm.

would have perished on a dry site.[14] A rotary quern was also found at this site as were billhooks and two small iron plough socks.[15] Grindstones and billhooks have also been found in ringfort excavations.[16] While tillage activity is evident, nowhere does it appear to have been the dominant economic activity of the ringfort dwellers.

A certain amount of manufacturing took place within ringforts, but the economic importance of this activity is uncertain. Weaving and the production of bone and antler objects were most likely carried on in the ringfort with production confined to meet the needs of its occupants. A tiny saw probably used in the manufacture of bone combs was found at Deer Park Farms,[17] while waste fragments from Lissue show that lathe-turned wooden objects were manufactured there.[18] There are a number of ringforts where excavation results suggest that the sites were permanent centres of craftsmanship and manufacture: Garryduff 1 and Garranes, Cork produced crucibles, stone moulds, glass rods, tongs and anvils,[19] whilst Clogher, Tyrone, the Early Christian royal site, seems to have been the location of a metal working centre which made a distinct type of zoomorphic penannular brooch.[20] De Paor believes that Ardagh functioned as a shelter for manufacture.[21] In Early Irish law, access to a mine is one of the locational factors which contributed to land values suggesting that most metalworking, especially iron working, was a widespread but small scale enterprise.

Despite the evidence for tillage and manufacturing, it can be concluded that ringfort dwellers were principally cattle farmers, and that dairying was their chief economic pursuit. By shrewd husbandry and successful clientship arrangements, their numbers of cattle were increased, and it was through cattle that their personal wealth and status was measured.

14 Lynn, 'Deer Park Farms', pp 11–15.   15 C. Lynn and J. McDowell, 'Deer Park Farms report project' in *IAPA Newsletter*, x (1989), pp 23–4.   16 Ibid., p. 24.   17 Ibid.   18 Proudfoot, 'Economy of the Irish rath', p. 116.   19 O'Kelly, 'Garryduff, pp 99–103; M. O'Kelly, 'The excavation of a large earthen ring-fort at Garranes, county Cork' in *Proceedings of the Royal Irish Academy*, xlvii (1942), C, pp 77–150, see pp 134–9.   20 Warner, 'Early historic Irish kingship', p. 66.   21 Barrett, 'The ring-fort', p. 136.

5 Environment

The essentials of the modern Irish landscape were in place from the outset of the Early Christian period which permits us to relate the settlement pattern of a thousand years ago to the conditions first mapped in detail in pre-industrial mid-nineteenth century Ireland. Much of the coastal rim, about 19% of the island, was dominated by inhospitable uplands. Blanket bog and upland gley soils formed a barrier to settlement in these regions, especially in the western counties of Kerry, Galway, Mayo and Donegal. Meanwhile, raised bogs were widespread in the low-lying, undulating glacial deposits which were often poorly drained. About 21% of the modern Irish landscape is still dominated by bogs or inhospitable upland,[1] and the Early Christian figure was undoubtedly much higher. Taking the island as a whole, the aforementioned physical conditions determined that settlement could not take place during the Early Christian period in about one-third of it. In addition, farming in a further 15% of the island was retarded by a band of drumlins curving from Strangford Lough in the north-east to Donegal Bay in the west which created a mosaic of poorly drained hillocks surrounded by waterlogged valleys.[2]

Woodland was a far less tenacious constraint on settlement but it must account for significant gaps in the distribution of ringforts. The earliest topographical maps of sixteenth- and seventeenth-century Ireland show a heavily wooded terrain with islands of cleared land.[3] While it is impossible to estimate the extent of woodland at the outset of the Early Christian period – a thousand years prior to the earliest maps of woodland cover – it is possible to chart the ebb and flow of woodland cover at individual locations using pollen analysis.[4] The pollen record has the advantage that, unlike the Early Christian written record, it is unbiased both geographically and politically; nor is it shrouded in the uncertainties of contemporaneity and uneven destruction rates which contaminate the study of settlement remains.[5]

Throughout Ireland, pollen cores give a remarkably similar account of Early Christian environmental history. As early as 1956, Mitchell highlighted the use of

---

1 Ordnance Survey, Ireland: general soil map (second ed., Dublin, 1980). 2 M. Gardiner, 'Land use capability' in Royal Irish Academy, *Atlas of Ireland* (Dublin, 1979), p. 28. 3 See maps of Laois/ Offaly (frontispiece) and Scarawalsh (plate A) reproduced in A. Smyth, *Celtic Leinster.* 4 4 The science of palynology reconstructs local vegetation on the basis of fossil pollen; it shows the species composition and extent of woodland and, where woodland is in decline the nature of the human interference, and the type of farming practised. 5 See chapter 6.

palynological research along with radiocarbon dating.[6] Detailed analysis of a pollen core at Littleton Bog, Tipperary typified the results which were to emerge from subsequent research.[7] Although there are no precise dates from this site, it appears that from $c.300$ BC to AD300 there was a lull in human activity which led to a resurgence in hazel and elm and a decline in those species which are associated with cleared land and farming activities (fig. 4). Around AD400, grasses, plantain, bracken and Artemisia (mugwort) reappear and cereal pollen becomes continuously present which suggests the growing importance of human activity.[8] A pollen core from Cashelkeelty on the Beara peninsula, Kerry indicated that the late Iron Age lull in arable activity ended there around AD590 when an upsurge in farming – and weed pollen associated with pastoral and arable farming – was accompanied by the introduction of oats (fig. 4).[9]

A different story is told in the pollen record of the agricultural land in the vicinity of Red Bog, Louth (fig. 5). Here the lull in human activity was earlier, dating from $c.800$ BC to AD25. Between AD25 and AD400, there was a sharp fall-off in hazel and oak along with the virtual extinction of elm locally. At the same time, grass pollen increased in importance and cereal was once again present. This clearance phase ended during the middle of the sixth century when most pollen diagrams show intense human activity.[10]

A more usual sequence was confirmed at nearby Essexford Lough (fig. 5).[11]11 There, the lull in human activity lasted until AD500 during which time tree pollen assumed 95% of the pollen sum. A major expansion in agriculture occurred from $c.$ AD500 accompanied by a comparable rise in *Plantago lanceolata* (ribwort plantain), cereal pollen increased along with a wide range of arable weeds including Artemisia. Included in the arable activity was the growing of oats which were introduced into Ireland during the Iron Age, perhaps early in – the first millennium AD.[12] Between AD540 and AD700, there was some regeneration of woodland but arable and pastoral agriculture indicators continue at high levels. From AD700 intense agricultural activity is again accompanied by a further decline in woodland; cereal values rise to 7%, which is very high, and rye and Cannabis are also recorded. The pollen record indicates that the vicinity of Essexford Lough remained intensely farmed through to the end of the millennium.

6 G. Mitchell, 'Post-boreal pollen-diagrams from Irish raised-bogs' (Studies in Irish Quaternary deposits: no. 11)', in *Proceedings of the Royal Irish Academy*, lvii (1956), B, pp 185–251.   7 G. Mitchell, 'Littleton Bog, Tipperary: an Irish agricultural record' in *Journal of the Royal Society of Antiquaries of Ireland*, xcv (1965), pp 121–32.   8 Ibid., p. 128, fig. 1.   9 A. Lynch, Man and environment in south-west Ireland, 4,000 B.C.–A.D. 800; a study of man's impact on the development of soil and vegetation (Oxford, 1981), see pp 83–4.   10 D. Weir, 'A palynological study of landscape and agricultural development in county Louth from the second millennium BC to the first millennium AD' in *Discovery Programme reports 2; project results 1993* (Dublin 1995), pp 77–126, see pp 91–2.   11 Ibid., pp 96–7. The interpretation that follows is at odds with Weir's account, which, for example, describes an expansion of hazel from 540 AD when it in fact declined   12 Ibid., p. 108.

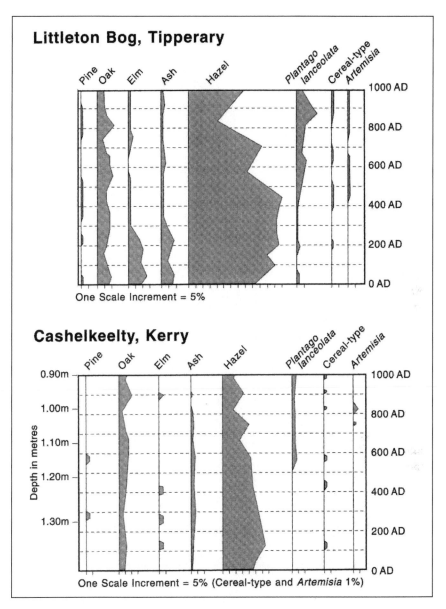

Figure 4   Simplified pollen diagrams from Littleton Bog, Tipperary (after Mitchell, 1965) and Cashelkeelty, Kerry (after Lynch, 1981) in the first millennium. At Littleton Bog the hazel decline is accompanied by a sharp rise in *Plantago lanceolata around* AD400 indicating an increase in pasture in the vicinity of the bog. At Cashelkeelty a less dramatic hazel decline occurs late in the sixth century, again accompanied by a rise in the pastoral indicator Plantago lanceolata.

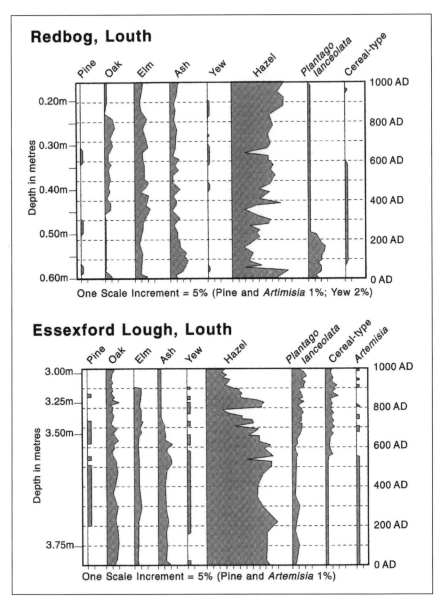

Figure 5   Simplified pollen diagrams from Louth in the first millennium. Different
conditions prevailed in the vicinity of Red bog than are usual for pollen
diagrams of this period: agriculture was most intense prior to *c.*AD25 although
cereal-type pollen is present to AD600. Nearby at Essexford Lough, the more
usual pollen sequence is apparent; hazel declines from AD600 and this is
accompanied by sharp rises in *Plantago lanceolata* and cereal-type pollen (after
Weir, 1995).

The pollen diagram from Lislarheenmore in the heart of the Burren, Clare is particularly helpful in understanding the environmental conditions of the ringfort occupants in the area as the sample was taken from a peat core in the immediate vicinity of an average-sized (34m in diameter) ringfort.[13] The vegetation history here parallels Mitchell's findings. A phase of intense human activity lasted from 1250 BC to AD200 (fig. 6). By this time tree pollen was at a very low level while cereals and pollen from pasture loving weeds were in abundance. The indication is that hazel-dominated scrub expanded once again and that agricultural indicators declined after AD200 due to a deterioration in soil conditions indicated by the accumulation of peat.[14] At *c*.AD580, later than in previously discussed examples, intense pastoral-based agriculture is once more in evidence. At Lislarheenmore, this change is preceded by a layer of silty clay which was probably washed down during the construction of a ringfort located on higher ground. Pasture expanded to such an extent throughout the Burren that yew and pine became extinct or almost extinct around AD600. Weeds that are indicative of arable farming do not, however, undergo an upsurge at this time due to the shallow soil cover on the local limestone and it is suggested, therefore, that pastoral-based farming dominated the economic pursuits of the inhabitants of the neighbouring ringfort.

At Lislarheenmore and throughout the Burren, the hazel decline around AD300 is a key indication of the upsurge in farming activity (figs 6–7).[15] This is accompanied by a rise in *P. lanceolata*. About the same time, the introduction of cereal in the pollen profiles indicates increased tillage activity which has been attributed by Mitchell to the introduction of the coulter plough.[16] The major expansion of agriculture also corresponds to a period of particularly warm and dry weather which may have lasted until about AD530.[17] Around AD600, there is a rise in Artemisia pollen, a weed which grows when competition from other weeds is reduced. Mitchell believes that this was a development favoured by the introduction of the mouldboard plough.[18] Weir, however, considers this explanation 'unlikely', instead attributing its rise to a land management system involving a fallow period.[19]

On the island of Inishbofin the Late Iron Age Lull, which commenced *c*.179 BC, ended in the beginning of the fourth century AD with an upsurge in woodland

13 L. Jelicic and M. O'Connell, 'History of vegetation and land use from 3200 B.P. to the present in the north-west Burren, a karstic region of western Ireland' in *Vegetation History and Archaeobotany*, 1 (1992), pp 119–40; M. O'Connell and L. Jelicic, 'Lias Lairthin Mór (LLM II), N.W. Burren: history of vegetation and land use from 3200 B.P. to the present' in M. O'Connell (ed.), *Burren, Co. Clare* (Irish Association for Quaternary Studies, field guide no. 18, Dublin, 1994), pp 54–71.   14 Jelicic and O'Connell, 'History of vegetation', pp 119–40.   15 Ibid., pp 133–4, fig. 8.   16 Mitchell, *The Irish landscape*, p. 153.   17 Weir, 'A palynological study', p. 111. Lamb maintains, however, that this period of improved climate ended *c*.400 AD; H. Lamb, *Climate, history and the modern world* (London, 1995), see p. 165. My thanks to Michael O'Connell for bringing this reference to my attention.   18 Mitchell, *The Irish landscape*, p. 162.   19 Weir, 'A palynological study', p. 109.

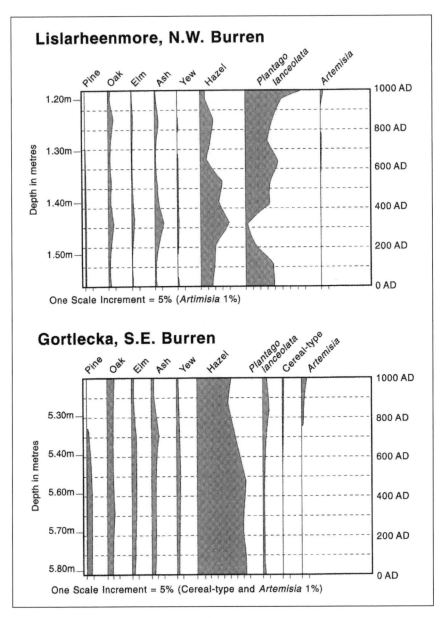

Figure 6   Simplified pollen diagrams from Lislarheenmore and Gortlecka, the Burren,
Clare in the first millennium. In the Burren, and elsewhere in Ireland, the hazel
decline is a key indication of the upsurge in farming activity. At Gortlecka,
the hazel decline was accompanied by a rise in *Plantago lanceolata*, declined
from *c*.AD100 but then increased dramatically from *c*.AD300 (after Jelicic and
O'Connell, 1992).

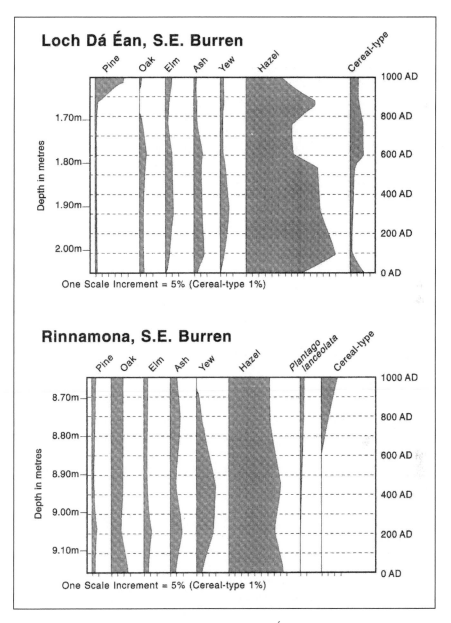

Figure 7   Simplified pollen diagrams from Loch Dá Éan and Rinnamona, the Burren, Clare in the first millennium. The hazel decline is very dramatic during the sixth century at Loch Dá Éan, as is the accompanying rise in cereal pollen. A dramatic rise in cereal pollen from *c*.AD600 at Rinnamona is associated with only a slight decline in hazel (after Jelicic and O'Connell, 1992).

clearance and pastoral activity. However, from *c*.AD575, Artemisia pollen is high while there is a contrastingly low occurrence of *P. lanceolata* pollen, indicative of arable-based Early Christian farming.[20] The shift to a tillage economy roughly coincides with the foundation of St Colman's monastery in AD665, and it is also significant that this absence of pastoral activity is coupled with the absence of ringforts on Inishbofin.[21]

The evidence of thirteen pollen diagrams throughout Ireland have been summarised by O'Connell, who, more than any other modern palynologist, concentrates on more recent (geologically speaking) Quaternary events (fig. 8).[22] In Ireland, the late Iron Age (to *c*.AD250) is characterised by a lull in human activity which permitted a regeneration of woodland and scrub. From AD250, however, this 'late Iron Age lull' was followed by a period of intense and prolonged human activity which left many of the sampled sites clear of woodland.

Related to woodland clearance, and linked to the expansion of population from AD250, is evidence of soil erosion. On the slopes of Forth Mountain in Wexford, a drainage trench revealed thin layers of organic material under 1m of soil. These deposits have been dated to *c*.AD500 and attributed to the construction of a ringfort and subsequent farming 600m upslope.[23]23 As was noted above, a similar phenomenon was observed in the pollen core from Lislarheenmore in the Burren, where a layer of silty clay in the peat deposits (dated to *c*.AD480) was associated with the construction of a nearby ringfort and intensive grazing.[24] There is further evidence of substantial soil erosion in many Irish lakes as a result of severe deforestation after AD300.[25]

In summary, a great expansion in agriculture occurred in Ireland commencing about AD250. This upsurge in activity corresponded with the introduction of new technology in the form of advanced types of plough and perhaps new methods of land management. Wheat, barley, oats and to a limited extent rye were either introduced or farmed at increased levels. Initially, the development in plough technology permitted more land to be brought into agricultural production. An increase in farming output, a prerequisite for population expansion, must have

20 M. O'Connell and E. Ní Ghráinne, 'Inishbofin: palaeoecology' in P. Coxon and M. O'Connell (eds), *Clare Island and Inishbofin* (Irish Association for Quaternary Studies, field guide no. 17, Dublin, 1994), pp 60–108, see pp 77–9. 21 M. Gibbons, 'Inishbofin: archaeology and history' in Coxon and O'Connell (eds), *Clare Island and Inishbofin*, pp 54–9, see p. 57. 22 M. O'Connell, 'Vegetational and environmental changes in Ireland during the later Holocene' in M. O'Connell (comp.), *The post-glacial period (10,000–0 B.P.): fresh perspectives* (Dublin, 1991), pp 21–5. 23 E. Culleton and G. Mitchell, 'Soil erosion following deforestation in the Early Christian period in south Wexford' in *Journal of the Royal Society of Antiquaries of Ireland*, cvi (1976), pp 120–3. 24 Jelicic and O'Connell, 'History of vegetation', p. 134, fig. 8. 25 M. O'Connell, 'Ireland' in B. Frezel (ed.), *Evaluation of land surfaces cleared from forests in the Roman Iron Age and the time of migrating Germanic tribes based on regional pollen diagrams* (Stuttgart, 1994), pp 50–4, see p. 50.

inevitably allowed a significant improvement in the health of the population and a warmer, dryer climate may also have contributed to this. A better diet and a healthier population led in turn to an increase in population necessitating greater land clearance and more produce and further increases in population. This cycle and rapid environmental change provides the background to the equally dramatic developments in settlement types and density discussed in chapter two which represented a marked discontinuity from the prehistoric Iron Age.

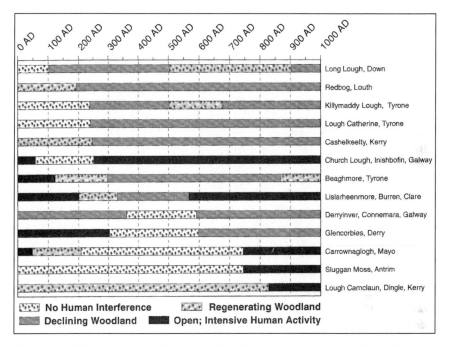

Figure 8   This summary of thirteen pollen diagrams shows how the 'Late Iron Age Lull' was followed by a period of intense and prolonged human activity from *c.*AD250) which left most of the sampled sites clear of woodland (after O'Connell, 1991).

6 Distribution

The importance of ringforts as an indicator of farm size and settlement density has been understood since early in this century when Westropp compiled statistics concerning all Irish fortifications and the number of acres per site.[1] The problem remains, however, as to whether or not the existing distribution of ringforts is a relict distribution or a real index of secular settlement during the Early Christian period. If one accepts, for argument's sake, that no site was built after the first millennium, there is a gap of eight hundred years between the apogee of ringfort occupation and their first accurate mapping by the Ordnance Survey in the mid-1800s. What happened, or did not happen, in the intervening period is the subject of much controversy and often lies at the heart of explanations of regional variation in ringfort density. There was no rationale for the destruction of ringforts in pastoral areas which characterised the greater part of Ireland before and after the corning of the Normans. They provided shelter for cattle, were protected by the widespread belief that they were the habitations of fairy folk and, in the centuries prior to the invention of the mechanical digger, would have required a great deal of energy to remove. In contrast, ringforts would have interfered with ploughing and, as areas of low ringfort density correspond to intensely-tilled, highly-Normanised areas, here it seems a valid assumption that many sites were destroyed during eight centuries of tillage.

O'Flanagan has attempted to assess destruction rates in the period immediately prior to the Ordnance Survey based on the estate maps of Bernard Scale.[2] Scale depicted seventy-three earthworks when he mapped the Duke of Devonshire's estates in Cork and Waterford in 1773, but the first edition OS 1:10,560 maps show only forty-two of these sites with just twenty being depicted on the 1937 edition.[3] At first sight, there appears to have been a 42% destruction rate of ringforts between 1773 and 1843–5, in which case there would be serious difficulties in regarding the distribution of sites as depicted by the Ordnance Survey as anything approaching

---

1 T. Westropp, 'The ancient forts of Ireland: being a contribution towards our knowledge of their types, affinities and structural features' in *Transactions of the Royal Irish Academy*, xxxi (1902), pp 579–730, see pp 586–8.   2 P. O'Flanagan, 'Surveys, maps and the study of rural settlement development' in D. Ó Corráin (ed.) *Irish antiquity; essays and studies presented to Professor M.J. O' Kelly* (Cork, 1981), pp. 320–6.   3 Ibid., p. 323.

the actual distribution of ringforts during the Early Christian period. Yet, the loss of information might not be as bad as all that: first O'Flanagan does not record to what extent the sites marked on the third edition are the same as those marked on the first; secondly, his study claims to refer to ringforts but also includes moated sites which have a notoriously high destruction rate.[4] Moated sites or 'square forts' seem to have been regarded as small fields and no taboos stood between them and their destruction. Both of the foregoing factors mitigate the actual ringfort destruction rate claimed by O'Flanagan.

Barrett describes a similar situation in her analysis of a 16km² area centred on the townland of Dunmanoge in the Barrow valley, south Kildare.[5] The Ordnance Survey recorded only one ringfort in this area. St Joseph discovered three new ringforts in 1971 and aerial reconnaissance by Barrett over three summers (1989–91) added five more probable ringforts, increasing the settlement density from 0.06 ringforts per km² to 0.56/km². The possibility that eight out of nine (89%) Early Christian settlements were removed from the landscape prior to Ordnance Survey mapping imposes serious limitations on distributional analysis in south Leinster and in other intensive tillage areas. But even in an area which has been intensively studied from the air over many years, the ringfort density just reaches the national mean. Questions also remain as to how representative this study area is as it was drawn to the attention of aerial archaeologists precisely because of its richness of cropmarks, and to whether or not intense aerial reconnaissance in an area of high ringfort settlement would produce similar new discoveries. In contrast to the findings in Dunmanoge, another study by the same author on the contribution of aerial photography in Louth established that new discoveries broadly replicated the distribution pattern of ringforts derived from OS maps.[6] Similarly, Proudfoot detected only a few new sites from aerial photography of Down, and believed that O'Donovan greatly exaggerated when he claimed that there had been a large number of ringforts destroyed prior to the Ordnance Survey.[7] In summary, I do not feel that there is conclusive evidence that pre-Ordnance Survey destruction rates seriously skew the existing distribution pattern.

In recent years, the Sites and Monuments Record (SMR) Office and other county surveys have made concerted efforts at examining aerial photography for settlement evidence destroyed before the arrival of modern cartographic methods in Ireland. Theirs was a more systematic approach to aerial reconnaissance and relied on the total coverage afforded by the vertical 1:30,000 Geological Survey of Ireland

---

4 For example, in the barony of Ikerrin, Tipperary only one of six moated sites survives; see G. Stout, *Ikerrin*, pp 122–3.   5 G. Barrett, 'Recovering the hidden archaeology of Ireland: the impact of aerial survey in the River Barrow valley, 1989–91' in *Forschungen zur Archäologie im Land Brandenburg*, iii (1995), pp 45–60, see pp 52–7.   6 G. Barrett, 'Problems of spatial and temporal continuity of rural settlement in Ireland, A.D. 400 to 1169' in *Journal of Historical Geography*, viii (1982), pp 245–60, see p. 256.   7 Proudfoot, 'Settlement and economy in county Down', pp 439–41.

photographs.[8] The SMR found that aerial photography consistently added *c.*10% to the number of mapped ringfort sites which goes some way towards restoring ringfort distributions to their 'original' level. Although new sites discovered from aerial photography were 4% more numerous in Leinster than elsewhere in Ireland, this difference is too small to significantly alter existing distribution patterns.

Table 2
The contribution of aerial photography to the SMR

County	Total sites	Sites from aerial photographs	Contribution
Carlow	767	73	9.5%
Dublin	1129	113	10.0%
Kilkenny	2234	216	9.7%
Offaly	1753	211	12.0%
Wexford	2209	261	11.8%
Wicklow	1321	145	11.0%
Leinster	*9413*	*1019*	*10.8%*
Leitrim	1620	130	8.0%
Waterford	1925	100	5.2%
Outside Leinster	*3545*	*230*	*6.5%*
Total	*12958*	*1249*	*9.6%*

Another systematic sampling method has a bearing on the reliability, or otherwise, of the existing distribution of ringforts as an indicator of their original number; this was the archaeological monitoring of the gas pipelines. Six pipelines have been constructed to date (fig. 9). The first runs from Kinsale to Dublin while subsequent work extended the network to Limerick, Mallow, Waterford, around Dublin and as far north as Dundalk. Prior to construction, a 1km wide corridor was marked on the OS maps and the proposed line was laid-out within these limits, to avoid all known archaeological sites. During construction, which involved scraping back soil from a 7m wide corridor, archaeologists investigated patches of darker soil which indicate buried features.[9] If it is true that the low density of ringforts in Leinster is attributable to a greater rate of pre-Ordnance Survey destruction, then it also follows that there would be a greater likelihood of discovering new sites in areas of low density. The gas pipeline construction project has not substantiated this hypothesis. The 220km

8 G. Stout, *et al.*, 'The Sites and Monuments Record for county Wexford; an introduction' in *Journal of the Wexford Historical Society*, xi (1986–7), pp 4–13; T. Condit and M. Gibbons, 'A bird's eye view of our past' in *Technology Ireland*, xii (1990), pp 50–4.   9 M. Gowan, *Three Irish gas pipelines: new archaeological evidence in Munster* (Dublin 1988), see pp 13–18.

long route from Cork to Dublin passed through areas of starkly contrasting ringfort density: densely settled west Kilkenny on the one hand, and Kildare and south Dublin on the other.[10] During the project, a souterrain was uncovered in south Tipperary, which in turn led to the discovery of a ringfort in a barony of above average density.[11] An Early Christian habitation site that was not a ringfort was found in south Dublin.[12] The 58km long pipeline laid from Mitchelstown to Limerick passed through areas of very dense settlement without hitting any ringforts. The 40km long Bruff to Mallow pipeline exposed what might be an isolated unenclosed Early Christian house, but no ringforts. The 50km long line from Clonmel to Waterford produced the same negative results despite passing through areas with varying ringfort densities.[13] Critically, the 75km long Dublin to Dundalk line, which passes through an uniformly sparsely settled area, had the same results.[14] The edge of a curvilinear ditch which might be a ringfort was revealed in Roganstown, Dublin but no definite ringforts were uncovered.[15] Two unenclosed occupation sites associated with souterrains, a common feature of Louth (and of Meath to a lesser extent), were detected at Smithstown, Meath and Dromiskin, Louth.[16]

Table 3
Early Christian sites discovered during construction of gas pipelines

Pipeline	Length	Ringforts	Other EC settlement
Kinsale/Dublin	220km	1	1
Mitchelstown/Limerick	58km	0	0
Bruff/Mallow	40km	0	1
Clonmel/Waterford	50km	0	0
South-west Dublin/Finglas	19km	0	0
Dublin/Dundalk	75km	1?	2

To summarise, while research in Cork/Waterford and Kildare has challenged the validity of the surviving ringfort distribution pattern, more systematic work

10 R. Cleary, M. Hurley and E. Twohig (eds), *Archaeological excavations om the Cork – Dublin gas pipeline* (1981–82) (Cork, 1987). **11** M. Hurley, 'Garrynatemple, Grange, county Tipperary' in Cleary, Hurley and Twohig (eds), *Cork – Dublin gas pipeline* (Cork, 1987), pp 65–70. Iffa and Offa East – 0.65/km². **12** M. Sleeman and M. Hurley, 'Brownsbarn, county Dublin' in Cleary, Hurley and Twohig (eds), *Cork – Dublin gas pipeline* (Cork, 1987), pp 71–3. **13** Gowan, *Three Irish Gas Pipelines* (Dublin 1988). **14** Bord Gais Éireann/M. Gowan, North-eastern pipeline, phase 1: report, archaeological monitoring of the construction phase (unpublished report, 1984); Bord Gais Éireann/M. Gowan, North-eastern pipeline, phase 2: inventory of all archaeological features and sites revealed during construction (unpublished report, 1989). **15** Bord Gais Éireann/M. Gowan, North-eastern pipeline, phase 2, p. 10. **16** Ibid., pp 31, 67.

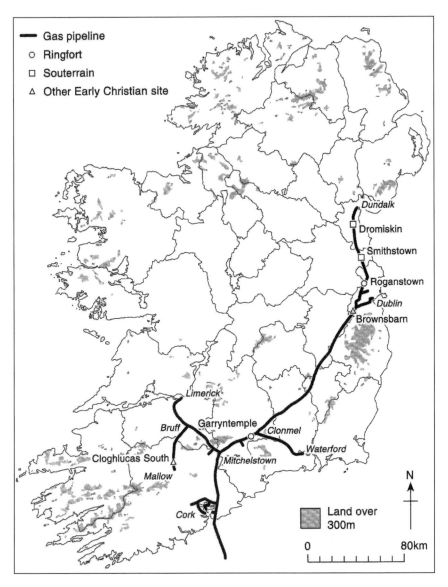

Figure 9   Although gas pipelines have passed through areas of widely varying ringfort density, they have not revealed more sites in low density areas.

undertaken by the Sites and Monuments Record Office and by archaeologists monitoring gas pipelines has shown that there is some justification for regarding the existing distribution of ringforts as being representative of the original Early Christian settlement pattern. I feel that the rate of destruction has not varied significantly by region; neither has it been so severe as to invalidate the map analysis which follows.

Taking the above considerations into account, it will never be possible to know the precise number of ringforts built in Ireland. Neither will it ever be possible to give a final total for the number of ringforts known in Ireland. The island's archaeology has only been surveyed in toto on a cartographic/aerial photographic basis. These preliminary surveys throw the net widely to include as many potential sites as possible which subsequent field work is designed to weed out. Field work, which has reached an advanced stage in twenty-six counties, excludes many of the 'enclosures' or possible ringforts noted during the cartographic and aerial photographic stage but at the same time adds many more sites discovered in the course of survey work. With destroyed sites, however, it will always be necessary to make an informed guess as to whether or not an enclosure marked on an OS map was in fact a ringfort or some other type of circular earthwork. The same subjectivity applies to circular enclosures detected only on aerial photographs.

Accepting these uncertainties, there are 47,337 ringforts in Ireland (up from 45,119 in 1995) of which 65% have been positively identified as of 2010 (up from 41% in 1995) (fig. 10). The mean density for Ireland as a whole is 0.55 ringforts per km², but this varies greatly: from below 0.20/km² in Donegal (0.15/km²), Kildare (0.18/km2) and Dublin (0 .19 /km2), to above 1. 00/km², in Roscommon (1.07/km²), Limerick (1.10/km²) and Sligo (1.61/km²). The regions of highest density are north Munster, east Connaught/north-west Leinster and east Ulster (fig. 11). Areas of low density are in north-west Ulster and most of Leinster. When examined on a barony-by-barony basis, variations in density and regional patterns become better defined. Densities of less than 0.10/km² are common in the western extremities of counties Donegal, Mayo and Galway, and also occur in parts of Meath and Kildare. At the other end of the scale, areas of very high density are centred on Sligo Bay (up to 2.17/km²), the Burren (up to 1.70/km²), central Limerick (up to 1.98/km²). The area of greatest concentration of ringforts in Ireland is the barony of Massereene Lower, Antrim, where there are three ringforts per square kilometre. The following analysis seeks to describe different regions of Early Christian settlement based primarily on ringfort density by barony units (figs 11–12). To keep the number of regions to a minimum, it has been necessary to ascribe some baronies to zones with slightly different densities.

ZONES OF LOW DENSITY

North-west Ulster is a region of low ringfort density (0.16/km²) which includes all of Donegal, and the western portions of Derry and Tyrone (fig. 13, plate 2). Ringforts are virtually absent above the 100m contour in the upland areas of Derryveagh, the Blue Stacks, Slieve League and the Inishowen peninsula. The barony of Boylagh, which includes the Rosses, has a density of only 0.03/km². Similarly, ringforts are very rare in the Derry/Tyrone uplands which include

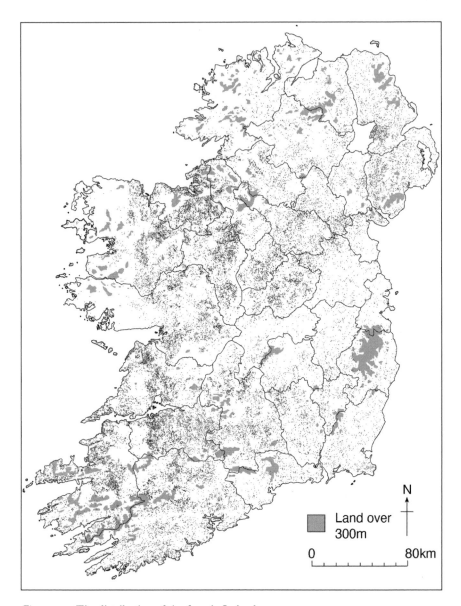

Figure 10   The distribution of ringforts in Ireland.

the Sperrin Mountains and the basaltic plateau west of the Roe River. These are agriculturally inhospitable areas of bare rock or thin drift developed from igneous rock. These factors together with the development of extensive blanket peat has effectively precluded settlement. Within this area of generally very low density, there are pockets of relatively higher density ringfort settlement. Most notable

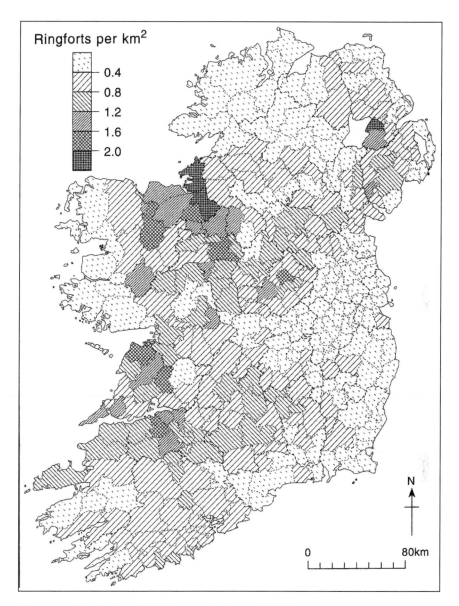

Figure 11   The density of ringforts per km² in each Irish barony.

in this regard is the low-lying carboniferous zone in south-west Donegal (see below). Ringforts are also present along the lower eastern slopes of the Derryveagh Mountains, the Roe River valley and the catchment area of the Mourne river centred on Bessy Bell mountain. Accepting that some Early Christian settlement is present, the area as a whole was relatively sparsely settled with ringforts despite

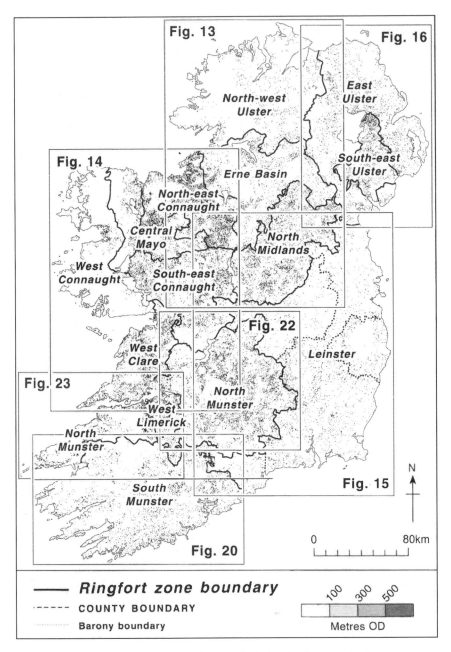

Figure 12   Key to figures 13–16, 20 and 22–23 depicting the fourteen ringfort zones.

Figure 13   Ringforts and places mentioned in the text in North-west Ulster, a zone of low
ringfort density; the Erne Basin, a zone of median ringfort density; and the
North Midlands, a zone of high density.

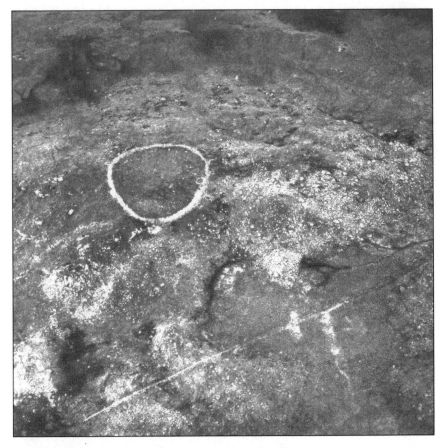

Plate 2   A large isolated cashel (stone ringfort) in Cashel townland, Strabane Upper, in
the Tyrone uplands south of the Sperrin Mountains (CUCAP BGQ 44).

the Mourne and Foyle river valleys being floored with acid brown earth soils with
wide agricultural capabilities. Other forms of secular settlement are also thinly
distributed in this area, although there is a sprinkling of souterrains sited in a
low-lying zone of good land between Derry and Raphoe. It must be assumed that
North-west Ulster maintained a low population density throughout the Early
Christian period.

Barrett examined ringforts in southern Donegal. She identified 174 sites[17] of
which 124 could be classified, in a study area reaching from Glen Head to Lough

---

17 No attempt has been made to make the numbers identified by field workers correspond to
the numbers identified in the Sites and Monuments Records and subsequent surveys.

Eske and south along the county boundary to Bundoran – taking in most of Tirhugh (0.27/km²) and Banagh (0.15/km²) baronies.18[18] This area had a diversified relief: low-lying plain around Finner, gently undulating land north and south of the Erne, hill topography in the extensive drumlin swarm extending eastwards from Killybegs, and valleys formed by rivers running southwards from the upland zone.[19] Thirty-two ringforts (26% of surviving sites) were cashels, and 15% were bivallate sites.[20] Ringfort builders avoided land below 30m, preferring land between 30m-60m, thought by the author to reflect the need for drainage and a better view.[21] Soil quality was statistically proven to be a key determinant of settlement density. Brown earth and grey brown podzolic soils were particularly favoured explaining the concentration of sites west of Donegal Bay. The brown earth soils and grey brown podzolic soils of St John's peninsula also attracted a higher proportion of sites than expected. In contrast, ill-drained, leached podzolic, gley and peaty soils were avoided, explaining the low densities on the poorer soils away from the coast.[22] The drumlin zone was avoided in preference to areas where the lime stone was overlain by thin glacial till.[23] The distribution of ecclesiastical sites corresponds broadly with that of ringforts with the exception of some monasteries, like that on Slieve League, which are obviously eremitic in character.[24]

West Connaught is a region of very low ringfort density (0.12/km²) in west ern Galway and Mayo (fig. 14). The lack of ringforts is readily explained by the inhospitable physical environment: bare rock in the Iar-Connaught lowlands, where densities do not exceed 0.05/km², gives way to the equally unattractive (from a farming standpoint) mountain region around Killary harbour, and further north, the blanket-peat covered wastes of north-western Mayo. The only break in this pattern is a scattering of ringforts found in a region of low-lying drumlins east of Clew Bay and extending onto the podzol soils of the rolling lowland east of Croagh Patrick. This inhospitable region did sup port some settlement, mainly ecclesiastical sites located on islands and main land coasts. Coastal shell middens from this period have also been identified. This coastal distribution reinforces the impression that the interior remained unsettled during the Early Christian period.

Leinster is the largest zone of low density (0.26/km²) making up twenty percent of Ireland (fig. 15). It takes in most of Leinster including all of counties Carlow, Dublin, Kildare, Wexford and Wicklow; large parts of Laois, Kilkenny, Louth, Meath, Offaly and Waterford; and baronies in Cork and Roscommon. The distribution of ringforts in this large area presents many difficulties in interpretation, the foremost being why there is such a low level of secular settlement in an area which includes some of Ireland's most productive soils.

18 Barrett, 'The ring-fort', table 3, p. 53; fig. 3, p. 24. **19** Ibid., p. 218. **20** Ibid., pp 64, 75. **21** Ibid., table 17, p. 218; p. 222. **22** Ibid., table 20, pp 227–31. **23** Ibid., pp 232–3. **24** Ibid., fig. 23, p. 257.

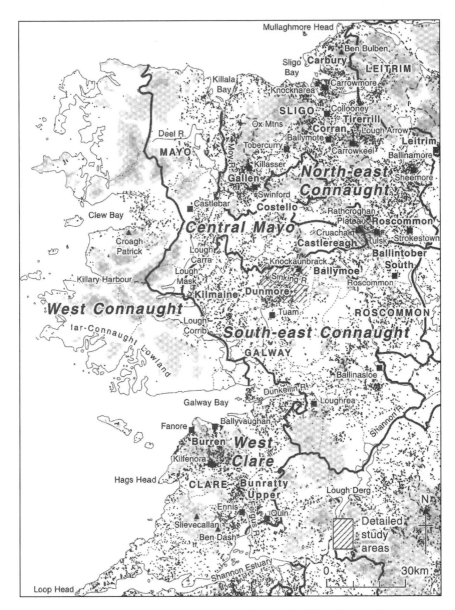

Figure 14   Ringforts and places mentioned in the text in West Connaught, a zone of
low ringfort density; Central Mayo, a zone of median density; South-east
Connaught, a zone of high density; and North-east Connaught and West Clare,
zones of very high density.

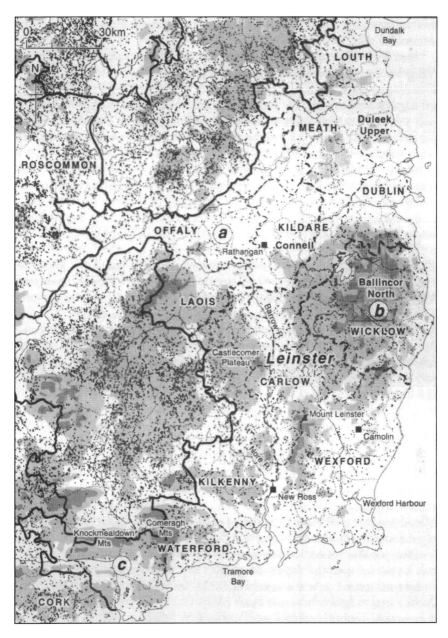

Figure 15   Ringforts and places mentioned in the text in Leinster, a zone of low ringfort density. Sub-zones a–c are areas where low density is attributed to adverse physical conditions.

Part of this pattern, however, is easily explained. **Leinster (a)**, which comprises parts of Offaly, Laois, Meath and Kildare, is covered by extensive areas of low altitude raised bog. The extent of bog cover would have been even greater during the Early Christian period prior to drainage works and peat harvesting which has intensified since the eighteenth century. Drainage has also removed large areas of fen which would have surrounded the raised bogs. Densities in this zone fall as low as $0.05/km^2$ in the barony of Connell in Kildare. **Leinster (b)** is the upland equivalent of the subzone just discussed. The mamillated slopes of the Leinster basolith are covered in blanket peat, an equally inhospitable environment as the waterlogged lowlands for the farming communities who inhabited ringforts. As a result, ringforts are virtually absent in the barony of Ballincor North ($0.08/km^2$) and very sparsely distributed along the lower altitudes of the five other baronies which surround the 500m plus granitic upland. To a lesser extent, physical features acted as a check on settlement in **Leinster (c)**. Here the Comeragh and Knockmealdown Mountains, the eastern extremity of the old red sandstone uplands, also pre vented high levels of secular settlement.

What remains of **Leinster** is a region of low density settlement stretching from Tramore Bay in Waterford to Dundalk Bay in Louth. Although the underlying geology may vary, the mantle of glacial drift here has produced soils of uniformly wide land use capability: acid brown earth soils in Louth and south Leinster; grey brown podzolic soils in Meath, Dublin and Kildare. Ringforts are least common in eastern Meath where densities fall as low as $0.04/km^2$ in the barony of Duleek Upper. There are, however, some notable concentrations of settlement: east of the Nore River on the lower drift covered slopes of the Castlecomer plateau in Kilkenny and Laois (the higher altitudes of these upper Carboniferous coal measures produce an inhospitable gley soil and consequently low ringfort densities); east of the River Barrow in Carlow and south Kildare; and lastly, on the lower south-east-facing slopes of Mount Leinster in Wexford, an area of sandy acid brown earth soils surrounding the southern limit of the long chain of granite upland.

One possible reason for the generally low density of ringforts is that this area coincides with the region of greatest and most durable Anglo-Norman settlement. Indeed, as it is a zone which remains Ireland's primary tillage producing area, ringforts here are more likely to have been gradually removed during eight centuries of intense tillage activity. This compelling argument is supported, as seen above, by the discovery of many destroyed enclosures in the Barrow valley and, for instance, in north Dublin and central Louth. Barrett and Graham, in an attempt to explain the distribution of ringforts in Meath ($0.28/km^2$), suggest that the continued construction of ringforts in the medieval period outside the area of Norman control and their destruction within that area helps to account for the comparatively small number of ringforts within the Norman zone. As has been shown, there is no evidence for medieval ringforts. However, statistics were used by Barrett and Graham to support the valid hypothesis that ringforts in north Leinster are more numerous in the north-west, and more specifically, that there were more ringforts within the Pale than without.[25] Many problems arise with their hypothesis: firstly, as there is a gradual reduction in ringfort density from north-west to south-east Meath, a line drawn anywhere on a north-east/ south-west axis would produce the same statistically significant results - results which may be related to a zone of Norman influence but could just as easily relate to a preference of ringforts builders for upland locations; secondly, it is just as probable that the Pale boundary, or more importantly, the Anglo-Norman frontier would have been constructed where ringforts, and the native Irish population they represent, were thinner in the first place.

In Louth (0.36/km²), Barrett returned to this theme and mistakenly interpreted the valid hypothesis of a difference in ringfort distributions on either side of the line of the Pale to provide evidence for a causal relationship which determined medieval and Early Christian settlement.[26] In addition, the most dramatic change in the distribution in Louth occurs well north of the suspected line of the Pale: ringforts are located in great numbers in the drumlin belt and on the lower slopes of the Cooley mountains (in **East Ulster**). This apparent predilection for upland areas is indicated in the avoidance by ringfort occupants of altitudes between 0m-31m, which accounts for a large percent age of the county, in spite of the fact that much of the lowland zone is an area of highly productive acid brown earth soils, the foundation of the present-day tillage economy in Louth.[27]

Bennett examined the distribution of ringforts in Wexford whose eight baronies all have very low densities (0.26/km²).[28] Wexford lies in the extreme south-east of Ireland with a variety of topography ranging from the granite uplands of Mount Leinster (796m) in the north-west, through an undulating intermediate zone (between 76m–230m) mainly in the west and north-west of the county, to a level lowland (below 76m) which is found near the coast and in the Slaney valley. There are a number of prominent hills (both topographically and historically) in the lowland zone. A wide band of acid brown earth soils stretches across the county from the north to south. Brown podzolic soils are present on the upper slopes of the Leinster chain, while along the east of the county gley soils predominate.[29] Ringforts are densest in a band along the edge of the granite uplands, and this is reflected in the preference for land between 76m–152m and an avoidance of land under 76m. The Wexford lowlands account for 65% of the total area of the county

25 G. Barrett and B. Graham, 'Some consideration concerning the dating and distribution of ringforts in Ireland' in *Ulster Journal of Archaeology*, xxxix (1975), pp 33–45. **26** Barrett, 'Problems of spatial and temporal continuity', pp 245–60. **27** Ibid., tables 4–5, pp 255–6. **28** I. Bennett, 'The settlement pattern of ringforts in county Wexford' in *Journal of the Royal Society of Antiquaries of Ireland*, cxix (1989), pp 50–61. **29** Ibid., pp 50–1, 56, fig. 3b.

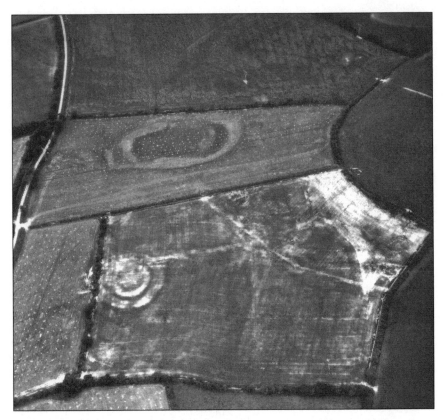

Plate 3   A pair of levelled ringforts show up as cropmarks south of Camolin in the
sparsely settled barony of Scarawalsh in north Wexford (CUCAP BGF 12).

but only 45% of ringforts are found in this zone (plate 3). Based on the present-
day distributions of both ringforts and soils, the light, easily-tilled acid brown
earth soils, which comprise 48% of the county's soil cover, attracted the lion's
share (73%) of Early Christian farmsteads. Sticky gley soils, which comprise
31% of the soil cover, were shunned with only 15% of ringforts being found on
these soils.30[30] Unlike Barrett and Graham, Bennett avoided reference to later
medieval destruction rates to explain the distribution pattern. This is borne out
by Anglo-Norman and late-medieval settlement (within towerhouses) as there
is considerable overlap between the zones of Early Christian settlement and
medieval occupation patterns, both of which are concentrated south of a line from
New Ross to Wexford Harbour.[31]

30 Ibid., pp 55–60, fig, 4a.   **31** B. Colfer, 'Anglo-Norman settlement in county Wexford',
in K. Whelan (ed.), *Wexford: history and society* (Dublin, 1987), pp. 56–101, see figs 3.8, 3.11.

ZONES OF MEDIAN DENSITY

East Ulster is a region of median ringfort density (0.35/km²) comprising eastern Ulster, but excepting **South-east Ulster**, the area of high density east and south of Lough Neagh (fig. 16). Within **East Ulster**, ringforts are concentrated in the lower altitudes. There is, for instance, a remarkably even spread of sites west of Lough Neagh and west of the rivers Blackwater and Lower Bann (plate 4). The upper limits of this settlement coincides with the 100m contour of the continuous upland area of Derry and Tyrone which includes the Sperrin Mountains. East of the Bann the settlement is also aligned along the 100m contour of the hills separating this valley from the Main Valley. These are areas dominated by gley soils but where sufficient drainage gives rise to acid brown earth soils which are not an impediment to farming. Elsewhere, there are places where physical determinants have precluded secular settlement: the basaltic plateau of north-east Antrim has extensive portions covered in blanket peat; the tertiary igneous Mourne Mountains; and the baronies of Oneilland East (0.01/km²) and West (0.12/km²) which coincide with the clay-floored flood plain south of Lough Neagh.

The two baronies of Lecale and the Ards peninsula in east Down also have unexpectedly low densities considering the highly productive acid brown earth soils in this region. Furthermore, Lecale has a high concentration of ecclesiastical sites including Downpatrick, the burial place of St Patrick. Low density of ringforts could be partly explained by the concentration of Norman activity and its associated intense tillage activity which could have destroyed ringforts in this portion of east Ulster, but an alternative explanation has been advanced by McCormick. As noted above, the high concentration of pig bones at Rathmullan in Lecale Upper may point to an intense tillage economy, perhaps dominated by ecclesiastical establishments, resulting in low cattle numbers which necessitated fewer ringforts.[32] Coastal Lecale has a marked concentration of souterrains which may also hint at a tillage-based economy, albeit of a slightly later date, where settlement within ringforts was of secondary importance. Evidence which suggests that the low density regions in **East Ulster** might be due to factors other than economic influences and/or Norman activity is suggested by the fact that in east Antrim the zone of lower density continues inland east of the Carn Hill uplands on the well-drained acid brown earth soils in the upper Six Mile Water valley. These are precisely sim ilar locational factors, if not even better from a soil perspective, as found in **South-east Ulster**, a zone of high density. Also, in the low populated areas of east Down, ringforts occur in groups of two or three just as they do in the more densely populated west of the county.[33]

---

32 McCormick, 'Farming and food in medieval Lecale'.   **33** Proudfoot, 'Settlement and economy in county Down', pp 454–6.

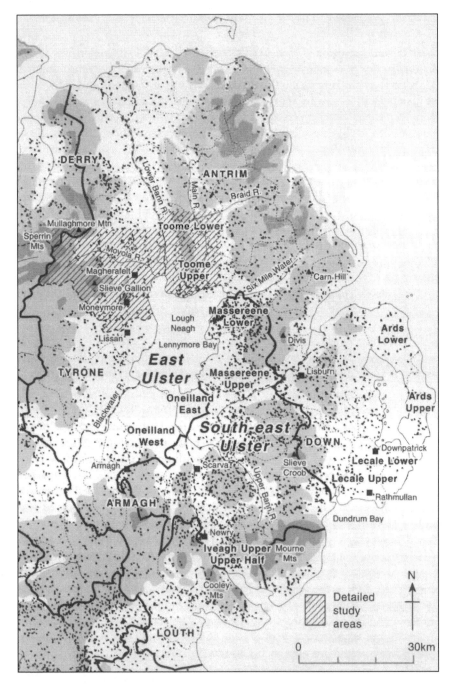

Figure 16   Ringforts and places mentioned in the text in East Ulster, a zone of median
ringfort density; and South-east Ulster, a zone of high density.

Plate 4   The ringfort at Lissan townland, Dungannon Upper, Tyrone is part of an even spread of sites west of Lough Neagh (CUCAP AVR 83).

Within **East Ulster** (and the high density area **South-east Ulster**) is found one of the greatest concentrations of souterrains in Ireland. In the barony of Ards Lower and extending south along the Main river valley, these underground chambers are in areas of lower ringfort density. North-east of Lough Neagh, however, souterrains and ringforts coincide. This inconsistent distribution pattern – complementary in some places, coinciding in others – makes it difficult to substantiate claims for a distinctive economic pursuit associated with souterrain concentrations or to argue for a chronology of settlement based on distribution evidence alone.

Speer has shown how physical determinants controlled the distribution of ringforts in the southern half of Loughinsholin barony ($0.46/km^2$) in south-east Derry. The area is bounded on the west by an arc of mountains from Slieve Gallion (529m) to Mullaghmore (556m), and on the east by Lough Neagh and the Lower Bann. Ringforts are restricted to median altitudes considerably below 180m (the limit of upland bog), and above 30m (the limit of lowland bog). There are three main concentrations of sites within the environmentally favoured region which reach densities of $4.00/km^2$: on the northwest facing slopes of Slieve Gallion, an area of light, sandy brown podzolic soils; on the western slopes of low hills formed on a limestone ridge east of Moneymore, an area of light, sandy acid brown earth soils; and a concentration north of Magherafelt aligned along a ridge of 60m plus hills bisected by the Moyola River, also in an area of light, sandy acid brown earth soils.[34]

Immediately east of the above study area, McErlean has examined Early Christian settlement north of Lough Neagh and east of the Lower Bann (fig. 17). This area, which includes most of the baronies of Toome Upper ($0.75/km^2$) and Toome Lower ($0.48/km^2$), is comprised of a basaltic upland, bisected by the Main River, and overlain mainly by gley soils. Drumlins, found in part of the study area, feature acid brown earth soils when well drained. Ringforts were located in loose groupings throughout the study area with as many as four sites in some square kilometres. Twenty-nine of thirty ecclesiastical sites were located at the margins of ringfort groupings or in clear isolation from secular settlement.[35] McErlean maintained that zones without ringforts, where one-third of the ecclesiastical sites were located, remained wooded to the end of the eighth century (fig. 18).[36] Two of the six ringfort groupings roughly correspond with parish boundaries, tentatively suggesting an Early Christian date for these territorial units.[37]

The **Erne Basin** is a region of median density ($0.45/km^2$) which includes all of Leitrim and Fermanagh, the Cavan 'panhandle' and parts of north Monaghan (plate 5), south Tyrone and north Longford (fig. 13). For the most part, the Erne Basin is underlain by limestone, but more importantly, it is a landscape of drumlins and inter drumlin lakes, especially Lower and Upper Louth Erne. These lakes are host to the densest concentration of crannógs in Ireland. This is a zone where the vagaries of drainage determines the farming potential of the gley soils. Ringforts are evenly distributed across wide low lying bands both sides of the Erne valley with arms extending either side of the Brougher mountain upland

34 D. Speer, 'The Early Christian settlement pattern in the south of the barony of Loughinsholin', unpublished BA thesis (The Queen's University of Belfast, 1982), see pp 2–18.   **35** T. McErlean, 'The Early Christian settlement pattern and structure in west mid-Antrim', unpublished BA thesis (The Queen's University of Belfast, 1982), see pp 6–15.   **36** Ibid., pp 41–3.   **37** Ibid., p. 28.

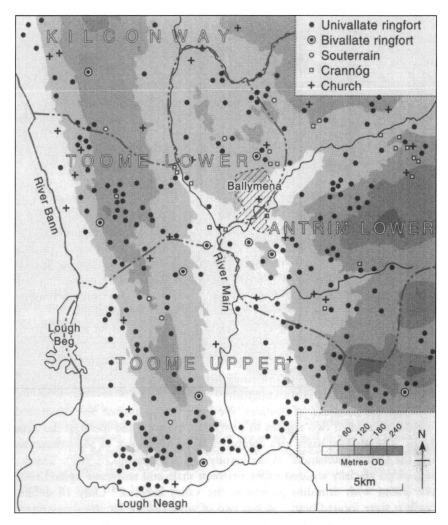

Figure 17   Early Christian settlement in south-west Antrim. Ringforts are most com mon
along the *c.*100m contour on the west-facing slopes of the Antrim plateau and
the upland lying between the rivers Bann and Main. Churches are found at the
margins of ringfort groupings usually at lower altitudes (after McErlean, 1982).

in a north-easterly direction towards the Clogher valley and the Ovenreagh river
valley to Dromore. Elsewhere, ringfort distribution is more patchy, It is very dense
in the Bonet river valley between Drumahaire and Manorhamilton (which is in
fact an extension of the dense Sligo groupings). Much of the Cuilcagh upland,
which dominates the Cavan 'panhandle', is devoid of ringforts, as is the raised
bog-covered landscape of south Leitrim/north Longford.

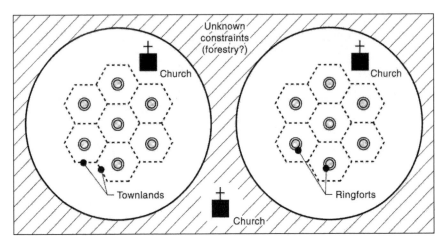

Figure 18   Model of Early Christian settlement based on a survey of south-west Antrim north of Lough Neagh. Ringforts are located in groupings within townland units. Churches are located either at the margins of these grouping or in areas lacking secular settlement. Unknown constraints on settlement, perhaps large areas of forest, account for areas without ringforts (after McErlean, 1982).

While the heartland of this area, the Erne valley, has not been examined, Farrelly has studied two regions in Leitrim in the west and south of the **Erne Basin**. The western study area comprises 60km² south-east of Manorhamilton near the Cavan 'panhandle' in the barony of Drumahaire (0.78/km²). This is a steep-sided glacially scoured valley between shale and sandstone upland rising over 300m with drumlins present in the valley bottom.[38] Only 18 definite ringforts were located here – all but two of which are in the low-lying northeast – giving a density of 0.30/km², well below the mean for the Erne Basin as a whole.[39] The mean distance to a ringfort's nearest neighbour was 738m which in terms of land holdings would have given an average of 152ha for each ringfort.[40] Despite the fact that over one-third of this area was over 213m, no sites were located in the upland zone. Consequently, ringforts avoided blanket peat which comprise 55% of this study area.[41] Eighteen percent of sites were bivallate ringforts and one-third of ringforts enclosed souterrains. Internal diameters tended to be smaller than the norm.[42]

In the southern study area examined by Farrelly, a 62km² area north-east of the Longford/Cavan border in the baronies of Mohill (0.26/km2) and Carrigallen

38 OS 1:10,560 sheet 12, see Farrelly, 'Sample study', fig. 9, p. 17; fig. 10, p. 19.   39 Ibid., p. 5.   40 Ibid., pp 45, 68.   41 Ibid., fig. 22, p. 52, p. 56   42 Ibid., p. 25, fig. 11, p. 28; fig. 16, p. 33.

Plate 5   Ringforts located on drumlins 10km east of Newbliss in the barony of Monaghan, Monaghan. Ringfort groupings noted in much of Ireland may not be present in drumlin zones were topography dictated an even spread of sites (CUCAP ALU 29).

(0.50/km²), drumlins dominate the low-lying limestone of the Rinn river valley, but an area of Ordovician upland (rising to 188m) is over lain by a thin layer of blanket peat.[43] Only 15 definite ringforts were located here giving a density (0.24/km²) again well below the mean for the Erne Basin as a whole.[44] The mean distance to a ringfort's nearest neighbour was 951m. In terms of land holdings, this would have given an average of 324ha for each ringfort.[45] These displayed a strong preference for land between 61m and 91m, with no ringforts located above 122m.[46] All of the sites were located north-east of the upland zone in the drumlin belt and two-thirds of ringforts were located on the crests of these drumlins on the better drained gley

43 OS 1:10,560 sheet 33, see Farrelly, 'Sample study' fig. 9, p. 17; fig. 10, p. 19.   **44** Ibid., p. 5.   **45** Ibid., pp 45, 68.   **46** Ibid., fig. 24, p. 54.

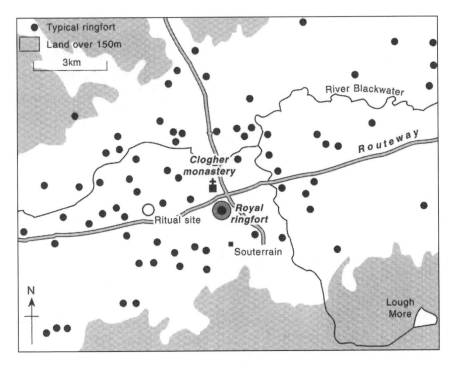

Figure 19   The royal ringfort at Clogher, Tyrone was located at the junction of two ancient roadways in the midst of a grouping of less imposing ringforts. Clogher and the nearby monastery formed the core of a diocese established in 1111 (after Warner, 1988).

soils.[47] 46% of ringforts were bivallate in an area of just over two square kilo metres. The clustering of bivallate sites means that this area does not correspond to the south-west midlands settlement model discussed below.[48] In this part of Leitrim, internal diameters tended to be larger than usual.[49]

Warner examined a 103.5km^2 area surrounding a royal ringfort in the barony of Clogher (0.47 /km^2), Tyrone. This is in a wide limestone floored valley below and north of Slieve Beagh (370m) and most of the ringforts are found below the 120m contour (fig. 19). The vicinity of Clogher has a density of 0.67/km^2, slightly above the mean density for the **Erne Basin** as a whole. The documented royal site, which had two banks but a contrastingly small interior, was located in a central place position at the junction of two ancient routeways in the midst of a grouping of less imposing ringforts and one isolated souterrain. In addition,

---

47 Ibid., fig. 3, p. 9; fig. 25, p. 55; p. 57.   **48** Ibid., pp 25, 46.   **49** Ibid., fig. 11, p. 28; fig. 16, p. 33.

Plate 6   Ringforts and early fields survive in unimproved pastureland 5km east of Ballyhaunis in the barony of Costello in Mayo (CUCAP ALR 96).

the royal ringfort was adjacent to an ecclesiastical centre and a ritual site.[50] This prominent ringfort clearly played a central place role in Early Christian Clogher valley settlement. While stressing that historical evidence alone can positively identify royal sites, Warner suggested that extrapolations could be made from Clogher evidence and the following factors could be used to identify high status enclosures elsewhere in Ireland; adjacent ritual mounds, small but heavily defended probably multivallate sites, and excavation evidence for wealth, large houses and mixed industrial waste.[51]

Central Mayo is an L-shaped zone of ringfort density slightly above the national mean (0.62/km²) (fig. 14, plate 6). It lies mainly in Mayo between the zone of low

50 Warner, 'Early historic Irish kingship', fig. 4, p. 66.   51 Ibid., p. 67.

density to the west (West Connaught) and the very high-density area of east Mayo/ north Roscommon (North-east Connaught), with an arm extending as far east as the upper reaches of the River Suck in Roscommon. This is mainly an area of low-lying drift-covered limestone which has produced grey brown podzolic soils with limited land use capability. Clusters of ringforts are found in the Deel valley to the east of the Moy River and in an area of drumlins between Castlebar and Lough Carra. The particularly high density of settlement here suggests that drumlins were, in this region, a positive attribute in the minds of the ringfort builders.

South Munster is a zone which, overall, has a mean density slightly below the national average (0.48/km²) (fig. 20). It comprises most of counties Cork and Kerry and is, therefore dominated by the ridge and valley topography of south-west Munster. It is an area where the old red sandstone has been folded, forming alternating lines of ridges and valleys orientated along an east/west axis. In the east, the valley bottoms are floored with limestone. North of Killarney the Devonian strata is overlain by a plateau of Namurian shale. The mountains are, naturally enough, devoid of settlement. In Kerry, for example, the northern portion of the Iveragh peninsula extending westward to the Macgillycuddy's Reeks are thinly settled; ringforts are rarest in the baronies of Iveragh (0.18/km²) and Dunkerron North (0.16/km²). The same applied in the westernmost limit of the Beara peninsula (Bear Barony 0.21/km²) and Carberry West WD (0.37/km²) in Cork. On the valley sides, however, ringforts occur in significant concentrations. Most notable is a band of sites on the warmer south-facing slopes of the Lee valley, from Ballyvourney (on the Sullane river) 15km west of Macroom extending eastwards to the south-facing ridge north of Middleton. Highly productive brown podzolic soils would have sustained the farming communities in this region. Another concentration of sites is found on the south-facing slopes of the upper reaches of the Blackwater valley, despite this being an area of predominantly gley soils. In south Cork, the anticlines reach heights of only *c*.150m and feature brown podzolic soils, permitting a cluster of sites at the top of the ridge between the Lee and Bandon rivers. Further south and west there are scatters of ringforts between Bandon and Skibbereen (plate 7).

Fahy examined the distribution of ringforts in Skibbereen Rural District, a 461km² area centred on the barony of Carberry West ED (0.59/km²).[52] The area extends from Roaring Water Bay to Glandore Harbour and reaches *c*.25km inland to Nowen Hill (537m). The drainage basin of the River Ilen forms the core of the area which is surrounded by old red sandstone upland on all but the seaward side. The flood plain of the Ilen extends 11km upstream from Skibbereen, but much of the lowland basin consists of gently rolling glacial deposits (derived from the local

---

52 E. Fahy, 'Early settlement in the Skibbereen area' in *Journal of the Cork Archaeological and Historical Society*, lxxiv (1969), pp 147–56.

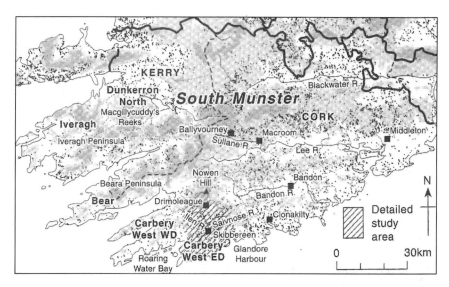

Figure 20   Ringforts and places mentioned in the text in South Munster, a zone of median
ringfort density.

sandstone) lying between 60m and 120m. Seventy-two percent of ringforts lie on
intermediate slopes between the 30m and 120m contours. The mean density of
this region is 0.51/km² rising to 0.71/km² in the vicinity of Skibbereen. Three-
quarters of ringforts within the rural district lie in four distinct zones each
featuring high quality, predominantly brown earth and brown podzolic soils: a
line of sites on the south-facing slopes below Nowen Hill just below and south
of the limits of blanket bog which roughly corresponds to the 180m contour; the
Saivnose river valley; the west side of the Ilen Valley at *c*.60m; and on the low,
rocky sandstone hills south-east of Skibbereen. Three areas, although they have
similar characteristics to the foregoing regions, are devoid of ringforts: the head of
Glandore harbour; east of the Ilen estuary; and a 65km² region of brown podzolic
soils south-east of Drimoleague. In the latter case, Fahy believes that the survival
of pine forests could have inhibited settlement, while the first area was too exposed
to the coast and/ or too low-lying to attract settlement. Fahy also maintained
that ringforts were arranged in two patterns; a linear pattern which mirrored the
influx of settlers into the area and a 'developed' pattern which indicated more
widespread colonising. It seems more likely, however, that the linear pattern was
imposed on the settlement by the morphology of the valley sides while non-linear
settlement took place in more level terrain.

Plate 7   A pair of large ringforts in low-lying terrain 3km east of Clonakilty in Carbery East (E.D.), Cork (CUCAP AVL 48).

ZONES OF HIGH DENSITY

South-east Ulster forms the north-eastern limit of a band of high to very high ringfort density which stretches from the eastern shores of Lough Neagh to Clare (**South-east Ulster, North Midlands, South-east Connaught, West Clare**). This diamond-shaped area with a high concentration of ringforts (1.05/km²) lies between Lough Neagh, Dundrum Bay, the Cooley peninsula and Armagh town, in contiguous parts of Antrim, Down and Armagh respectively (fig. 16). Drumlin topography accounts for most of this zone except for the baronies of Massereene Lower and Upper east of Lough Neagh. Soils are varied but acid brown earth soils account for much of the area. Wet gley soils derived from a basaltic till underlie much of the western portion of the Massereene baronies; yet they have the highest ringfort density in Ireland (over three sites per square kilometre). Here ringforts are found in two dense groupings; along the shores of Lough Neagh between Lennymore Bay and Six Mile Water, a particularly unusual concentration given that it lies below 60m; and on the west-facing slopes of the Divis uplands especially between the 91m and 183m contours. Another concentration of ringforts in this densely settled zone is found west of the Slieve Croob uplands between Lisburn and Newry where gley and acid brown earth soils predominate. In Scarva townland (Iveagh Upper, Upper Half – 0.79/km²) ringfort densities reach as high as eight sites per square kilometre.[53] Neither soils or siting seem to have influenced the distribution pattern in this area because, even in the drumlin belt, settlement density falls from south-west to north-east.[54] Settlement to the south of this zone is aligned along the 100m contour surrounding the lower slopes of the Cooley mountains in Louth, a zone of well drained acid brown earth soils.

North Midlands continues the band of high density from south Monaghan through Meath, Cavan, Longford and Westmeath to the Shannon (fig. 13). The northern portion of this area – north of a line running approximately from Nobber to Longford – lies in the drumlin belt and is, consequently, underlain with gley soils whose land use capabilities are limited by water log ging in some areas and by overly steep slopes in others. South of this line, the topography is dominated by undulating glacial kames. The sharply defined boundary between this zone and low density **Leinster** coincides with Westmeath's south-east boundary, corresponds with the limit of kame topography, and exactly picks out land lying over 100m. Most of this southern portion is underlain by highly productive grey brown podzolic or shallow brown earth soils. Ringforts are relatively evenly spread throughout the **North Midlands** (0.81/km²) but very high densities are achieved in central Westmeath, for example at Rathconrath (1.21/km²) and Corkaree (1.67/km²) west and north-west of Mullingar respectively (plate 8).

No sharper edge exists between areas of high and low ringfort density than that boundary which separates the **North Midlands** from low-density **Leinster**. At first glance, this suggests a demarcation based on the north east/south-west orientated limit of Anglo-Norman settlement. However, only the northern portion of the **North Midlands** (in the drumlin zone) respects the limit of Anglo-Norman occupation. Westmeath/East Longford has very high settlement densities from both Early Christian and medieval periods, which substantially weakens the argument that post Anglo-Norman destruction accounts for contrasting ringfort densities either side of this boundary. Whereas the drumlin belt marks the outer

53 Proudfoot, 'Settlement and economy in county Down', p. 456.   **54** Ibid., pp 456–8.

Plate 8   Three ringforts in Loughanstown townland in the densely settled barony of
Corkaree, Westmeath. EU grants during the 1970s facilitated the removal of
much of this rich grassland archaeology (CUCAP AVO 61).

limit of Anglo-Norman settlement, farmers in earlier times made use of both
drumlin zones and kame and kettle topography, while at the same time avoiding
the low-lying boulder clays of central and south Leinster.

The barony of Morgallion (0.68/km²) in the extreme north-east of this zone of
high density has been examined by Brady (fig. 21).[55] The barony has two distinct
topographic zones: in the north is the drumlin region while in the south is a
limestone and shale lowland. The drumlin readvance moraine forms the boundary
between the drumlin and lowland zones. Shale-covered drumlins are found north
of the River Dee giving rise to gley soils, but south of the river, drumlins are
overlain with limestone drift and a highly productive grey brown podzolic soil

---

55 Brady, 'Morgallion, country Meath'.

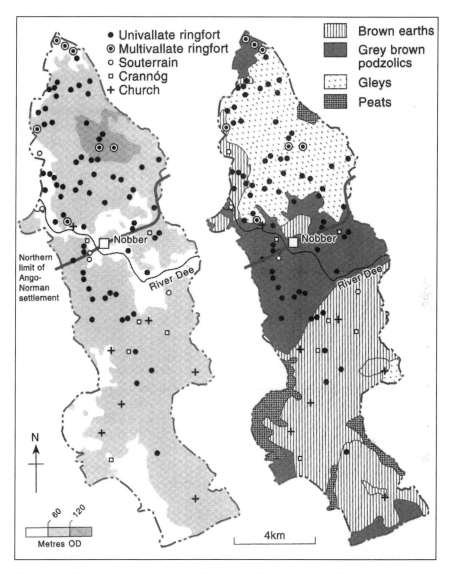

Figure 21 The distribution of Early Christian settlement in Morgallion barony, Meath. Ringforts are most common on grey brown podzolic and gley soils in the drumlin zone. Churches are more common on the brown earth soils of the kame topography in the south of the barony. There is some overlap between the area of densest ringfort settlement and Anglo-Norman settlement, suggesting that the low number of ringforts in the south should be attributed to reasons other than medieval destruction rates (after Brady, 1983).

cover has developed. Peat and water logged gley soils are found between the drumlins. The lowland zone is a poorly drained kame and kettle landscape giving rise to the development of raised bog to the east and west of the southern portion of this barony. Between these two extremes is a large expanse of brown earth soils.[56] In the north of the barony, ringforts are dense (1.07 /km² excluding bogland) and evenly scattered, and all of the multivallate sites are found here. In the south, ringforts are less dense (0.44/km²), and lie in a linear pattern dictated by the distribution of bog. Only 5% of ringforts (and just 9% of all Early Christian sites) are found below 61m, a lowland zone which comprises 18% of the study area. The Dee valley, where five crann6gs are located, has most of the multivallate sites and settlement within crann6gs roughly corresponds to the southern limits of dense ringfort occupation.[57] However, while crann6gs are found below 61m, all of the ringforts with two or three banks lie between 61m and 122m.[58] Most souterrains and ecclesiastical sites are found in the southern region.[59] Surprisingly, ringfort siting actually shows a strong preference for the gley soils of the drumlin belt rather than the brown earth soils of the southern low-lying region. Brady highlights one settlement locus where a church site – thought to have been the original location of a high cross base now located in Nobber – and a trivallate ringfort are adjacent to the only fording place on the River Dee in this region. This strategic location could explain the later development of the medieval town of Nobber.[60]

To Brady, the foregoing distribution indicates that a livestock economy was dominant in the shale-covered drumlins where most of the ringforts are found; certainly, it is a region where arable farming would have been difficult. In the limestone-covered drumlins and in the Dee valley, Brady proposes a mixed farming economy with a greater amount of tillage famung going in the valley. However, settlement differs from the livestock economy zone only to the degree that crann6gs are present. In the low-lying area of the barony, only 10% of ringforts are found in contrast to 86% of ecclesiastical sites and two thirds of known souterrains. Brady suggests that ecclesiastical sites could have relied more heavily on arable farming, making full use of lay monks on extensive church estates. Thus the south of the barony was an area where tillage was the main agricultural focus of a more nucleated settlement pattern, where ecclesiastical sites acted as population cores.[61] Critically, Brady attributes anomalies in the distribution of Early Christian settlement not to intrusive external elements but rather to varying economies dictated by the suitability of differing locations.[62] The medieval frontier crosses though the middle of the lime stone-drift covered drumlin belt *c.*3km north of the end moraine marking the limits of the kame and kettle lowland, not along the end moraine itself which Brady points to as the significant boundary between areas of high and low ringfort/ecclesiastical centre density. Once again, overlapping areas of high density Early Christian

56 Ibid., p. 10.   57 Ibid., p. 8.   58 Ibid., p. 13.   59 Ibid., p. 9.   60 Ibid., p. 27.   61 Ibid., pp 19–24.   62 Ibid., p. 33.

and medieval settlement do not support the view that Anglo-Norman settlement had a profound influence on ringfort distribution patterns.

South-east Connaught continues the band of high density ($0.78/km^2$) west of the Shannon river into south Roscommon and east Galway (fig. 14). Kame topography also continues here, albeit at ever lower altitudes in the Shannon and Suck river basins. Grey brown podzolic and shallow brown earth soils underlie the zones of densest ringfort settlement. Overall, the distribution of ringforts is more

Plate 9   An impressive multivallate ringfort found in typical proximity to a small univallate site in Turin townland in Kilmaine barony, Mayo. Despite the vastly different sizes of these two ringforts (and presumably the status of their occupants), the functional area of the ringforts is quite similar (CUCAP BDN 95).

patchy than in the North Midlands due to areas of bogland, especially in the Suck valley, west of the northern limits of Lough Derg, and along the flood plains of the Shannon. The main concentrations are found in an arc running from Roscommon town through Ballinasloe to Loughrea, and in an area to the north and west of Tuam, extending into the barony of Kilmaine (1.28/km2) in south Mayo (plate 9), bordered on the west by the Corrib-Mask-Carra lake system.

Neary examined the catholic parish of Dunmore in the north of this region. This is an area of approximately 150km² straddling the boundary between Dunmore (1.07/km²) and Ballymoe (0.83/km²) baronies in north Galway, in undulating glacial terrain (including eskers) with a thin soil cover which permits streams to sink into the underlying karst, a phenomenon which accounts for the name the Sinking River applied to the stream which bisects the study area from east to west. There are 159 ringforts in the parish giving a mean density of 1.06/km². Neary's distribution map highlights the complexity of the landscape; areas of bog are interspersed with areas of good land where ringforts are found. The area of densest ringfort settlement is found on the slopes of Knockaunbrack, in the north-west of Dunmore parish. The eleven multivallate ringforts (7%) are evenly spread throughout the parish. Neary believes that the distribution pattern was based on the strategic needs 'of a long vanished martial race of fort-dwellers'. Areas without ringforts were attributed to those places defended by natural features of else by 'hill-forts which compassed them'; an argument for the military function of ringforts and, unsustain ably in my view, a large population in unenclosed settlements.

North Munster is an area of high ringfort density (0.80/km²) stretching from western portions of Offaly, Laois and Kilkenny, and taking in all of Tipperary and Limerick except that part falling within **West Limerick**, an area of even higher density. It extends into the three north-western baronies of Kerry (figs 22–3) and into north Cork and Waterford. Geological influences account for the interruptions in this area of otherwise high density: the old red sandstone spine of the Dingle peninsula (Corkaguiney); the Namurian shales of north Kerry; and the Silurian uplands of the Silvermines and Galtee mountains are all devoid of ringforts. Elsewhere, despite variations in geology, the soil cover consists of highly productive grey brown podzolic soils in Tipperary and Limerick and brown podzolic soils in Corkaguiney off the mountain slopes. Some ringforts are located on the less hospitable gley soils in northern Kerry west of Listowel. Notable concentrations of ringforts in this densely settled zone include: the baronies of Clanwilliam (1.03/km2) and Middle Third (1.02/km²) in the Golden Vale of south Tipperary; the barony of Upper Ormond south-west of Nenagh; the upland known as the Devilsbit mountain which corresponds to the south-western portion of Ikerrin (0.93/km²); the barony of Galmoy in north-west Kilkenny (1.01/km²); and the concentration of ringforts along the south-facing slopes of the Dingle peninsula. The band of very high density in the western portions of Shanid and Glenquin baronies in Limerick are considered below in the discussion of **West Limerick**

Figure 22 Ringforts and places mentioned in the text in North Munster (eastern section), a zone of high ringfort density.

Ringforts are most common in **North Munster** from north Tipperary, to south Tipperary/west Kilkenny, and to central Limerick and their distribution coincides with one of the densest zones of Anglo-Norman settlement in the form of boroughs, markets and moated sites which are indicative of entrenched medieval occupation. The superficial observation that the area of lowest ringfort density (**Leinster**) corresponds to the zone of most intense Anglo-Norman occupation ignores, and is somewhat invalidated by, this remarkable area of settlement overlap. Neither can it be maintained that this zone of coincidence was outside the tillage area; records from the manor of Lisronagh in the barony

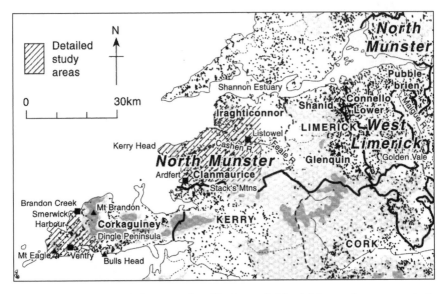

Figure 23   Ringforts and places mentioned in the text in North Munster (western section),
A zone of high ringfort density; and West Limerick, a zone of very high density.

of Iffa and Offa East (0.6S/km²) in Tipperary clearly detail a region where there
was classical medieval manorial farm management featuring the three-field
production of wheat and oats.[63]

The baronies of Ikerrin, Tipperary and Clonlisk, Offaly (0.55/km²) lie at the
northern limits of this zone of high density and have been the subject of exhaustive
research made possible by a pre-existing, detailed archaeological survey, undertaken
by G. Stout as part of a youth training scheme in the Roscrea Heritage Centre.[64]
The survey archive includes descriptions of the location of 314 sites and a largescale plan and section of all 206 surviving ringforts. Ten working years went into
the compilation of the survey and freed, for the first time, subsequent analysis from
the necessity of compiling field data.[65] The baronies have a varied topography as the
area they encompass lie either side of an inlier of old red sandstone orientated along
a northeast/south-west axis. The upland reaches its greatest altitude in the south-
west at the Devilsbit Mountain (463m). Grey brown podzolic soils predominate
on the well-drained slopes and foothills of this inlier. The solid geology of the
remaining area is lower carboniferous limestone overlain by sands and gravels;
morainic material has been deposited well above the 152m contour. Off the slopes

63 E. Curtis, 'Rental of the manor of Lisronagh, 1333, and notes on 'betagh' tenure in
medieval Ireland' in *Proceedings of the Royal Irish Academy*, xliii (1934), C, pp 41–76.   **64**
G. Stout, *Ikerrin*, pp 1–5.   **65** M. Stout, Ringforts, p. 203.

there is an undulating poorly-drained terrain upon which extensive peatlands have formed – over one-fifth of the study area is under bog. Ringforts are found in greatest numbers on either side of the drift-covered upland and are scattered more thinly in the non-bog areas of the remaining lowland: 54% of the study areas lies below 91m but only 24% of ringforts are found there; on the other hand, altitudes up to 273m were favoured by the ringfort builders. In Ikerrin, where detailed soil maps were available on a 1:10,560 map base, ringforts were fairly evenly distributed over all soil types, including the gley soils, except for an avoidance of peat and small pockets of rendzina soils.[66] Grey brown podzolic soils constituted 34% of the barony not covered by bog and 37% of ringforts were found on this soil type. Gley soils, where one could have expected to find fewer enclosures, constituted 37% of the barony and underlay 34% of ringforts; thus displaying no very dramatic preference for better quality soils.

The pre-existing survey made it possible to analyse ringfort distribution beyond these general environmental determinants. Fourteen variables from all surviving ringforts – relating to morphological, locational and distributional characteristics – were acquired to develop a classification of sites using a multivariate statistical process known as cluster analysis. As the issue of where to build a ringfort and how big to build it must have been foremost in the minds of the ringfort builders, it was felt that the computer would generate a mathematical surrogate for the mental maps which influenced past decisions. This technique identified five ringfort classes which had many similarities to classifications already devised for ringforts in Down and to a lesser extent, the barony of Clogher, Tyrone.[67] In the south-west midlands, it was found that a group of bivallate sites with small interiors (cluster 2), clearly the residences of high-status individuals, were located near groupings of smaller ringforts in upland settings (cluster 5). On the lower slopes and in strategic locations, ringforts with large diameters and impressive defences were found (cluster 4). In the low lying areas, ringforts tended to be more isolated from one another and were commonly raised above the level of the surrounding poorly-drained countryside (cluster 1). Finally, more typical single-banked ringforts were found strung out along well-drained slopes but in less strategic locations, often within their own townlands, and seemingly independent from other ringfort groupings (cluster 3).

Detailed study of six areas measuring 13.64km² within the two baronies highlighted the relationships between individual ringforts, territorial divisions and topography, which was the basis of the computer determined classification. Two examples illustrate the findings. Just south-west of Roscrea town, the ground rises sharply forming the upland known as Carrick Hill (fig. 24). Much

---

66 G. Stout, *Ikerrin*, fig. 23, pp 29–31. To my knowledge, this is the only study which related ringfort settlement to soil quality mapped at the most detailed level afforded by the National Soil Survey of Ireland.   67 Jope (ed.), *Survey of county Down*; Warner, 'Early historic Irish kingship', p. 67.

Plate 10   Three small Cluster 5 ringforts in the uplands of Killoskehan townland,
               Tipperary. A group of cattle on the right of the photograph indicates the
               number of animals which could have been accommodated within a ringfort in
               addition to domestic buildings (Brian Redmond).

of this area of well drained drift rises above 182m. The north-west slope is
very steep while the sheltered, south-east-facing slopes are more gradual and
support luscious pastureland. As expected, of the eighteen ringforts (1.32/km²)
here most are located on the south-east facing slopes. Ballycrine townland forms
the centre of one ringfort grouping which has, at its core, two bivallate sites
and a large enclosure which was probably an ecclesiastical site. At the summit
of the ridge and on the steep north-western side are four small ringforts and
two others which are now destroyed but appear to have been minor sites on the
basis of the OS designations. A similar juxtaposition of bivallate ringfort, small
sites and an ecclesiastical enclosure (1.5km distant off the map in Rathnaveoge
Lower) occurs on the ridge in the south-west of the study area. Between these
groupings which could be seen as two independent farming units are three very
large well-defended ringforts.

The second micro study area is located on south-facing slopes below the
Devilsbit Mountain centred on the townland of Killoskehan (fig. 25). It was
densely settled with 26 ringforts (1.91/km²). At 182m there is an impressive
bivallate ringfort (formerly conjoined with two smaller enclosures) and there
is another bivallate ringfort at 243m. Between these two impressive sites,
there are eight small ringforts (plate 10). On the lower slopes there are typical,

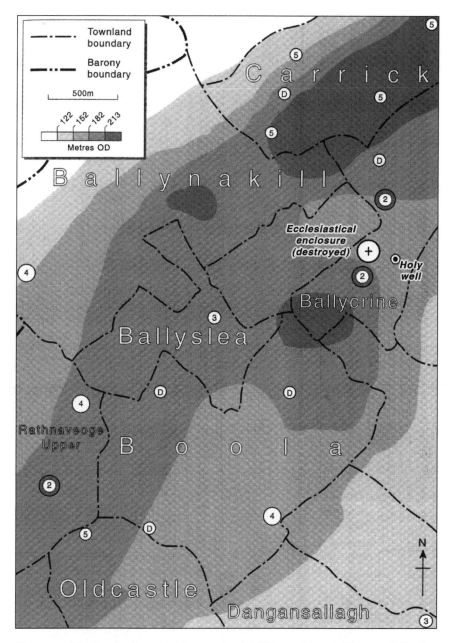

Figure 24   The distribution of ringforts on Carrick Hill, south-west of Roscrea. Ballycrine townland forms the core of one ringfort grouping 'separated' from another at Rathnaveoge by three large 'multi-functional' (Cluster 4) ringforts. The ringfort at Dangansallagh is one of a line of 'typical' ringforts (Cluster 3) strung out along the lower slopes between Carrick and The Devilsbit Mountain.

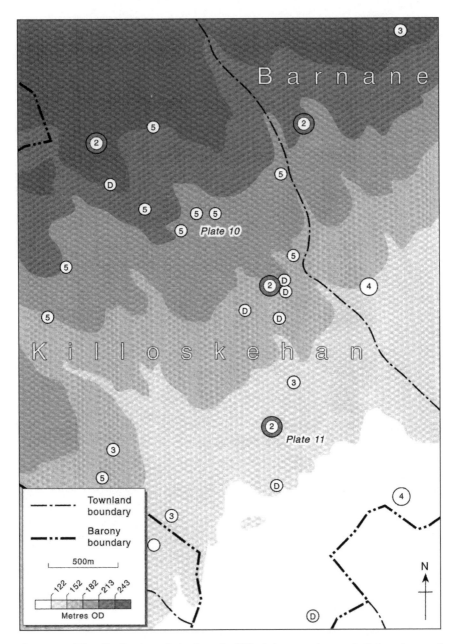

Figure 25   The distribution of ringforts in Killoskehan on the south-facing slopes of
the Devilsbit Mountain. A group of nine small upland ringforts (Cluster 5)
lie between two 'high-status' bivallate ringforts (Cluster 2). Large ringforts
(Cluster 4) are located in strategic positions on barony and townland boundaries.

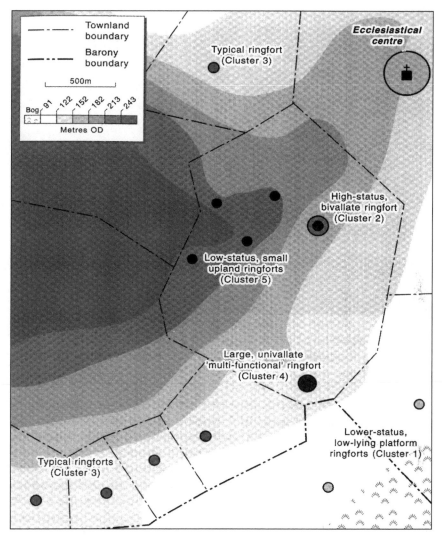

Figure 26 This normative model of ringfort distribution summarises the results of detailed spatial analysis in the south-west midlands. A high-status ringfort (Cluster 2) is found in close proximity to a group of upland sites with small interiors (Cluster 5). The 'high-status' ringfort is located near an ecclesiastical enclosure in a position to afford protection to the less significant upland enclosures. Downslope, a large 'multi-functional' ringfort (Cluster 4) is located at the edge of the townland/barony boundary. Segregated from the larger ringforts, but in close proximity to one another, are four 'typical' sites (Cluster 3). These are strung out along the 122m contour on good land that is less strategically placed. Two platform ringforts (Cluster 1) are located in relative isolation in a level, low-lying position.

Plate 11   A high-status Cluster 2 ringfort in Killoskehan townland, Tipperary. This site
             lies downslope from the smaller Cluster 5 ringforts (Brian Redmond).

single banked examples, and one bivallate platform ringfort with associated
earthworks (plate 11). Finally, near the barony boundary, which is conceivably
an ancient division, there is a very large and well defended ringfort in a
strategic location. The same pattern is repeated in Barnane townland on the
opposite side of a deep ravine which would have been a significant barrier in
the Early Christian period. Unlike the Carrick Hill study area, there are no
ecclesiastical sites located in this region.

A normative model provides a synthesis of the statistical results for both
baronies and for the detailed study areas in which 40% of the ringforts in the
two baronies were carefully considered (fig. 26). The typical density for the
south-west midlands is 0.95/km², which compares well with the mean density
for all of **North Munster**, and suggests that conclusions based on these two
baronies may be applicable to the wider zone. The foregoing results suggest the
following general picture. In a large townland, there is a 'high status' bivallate
ringfort in close proximity to a group of upland sites with small interiors. The
bivallate ringfort is also located close to an ecclesiastical centre. Downslope,
a large, well-defended ringfort is located at the edge of the townland/barony
boundary. Segregated from the prominent sites but in close proximity to one
another are four typical sites each within their own townlands. These are strung

out along the 122m contour on good land, but land that is less strategically located. Finally, two platform ringforts are located in relative isolation in a very level, low-lying position. The distribution and inter-relationships of different types of ringfort strongly suggest a hierarchical society made up of farmsteads mirroring classes of small, poor, independent, and highstatus families (see below, chapter 7).

Further north, in Offaly the south-west midlands settlement model does not appear to apply. The baronies of Ballyboy (0.45/km2) and Eglish (0.40/km2) form a marginal region of below average ringfort density lying between this zone of high density and the very low density **Leinster**. The percentage of high status ringforts is nearly three times the number expected from the above model and given the number of high status ringforts throughout Offaly. The probable reason for this contrasting distribution pattern is that Ballyboy and Eglish lie on the much-contested borders of six religious dioceses (Meath, Kildare, Clonmacnoise, Clonfert, Roscrea and Ossory) and four, provinces (Meath, Leinster, Connaught and Munster). We know from the lives of the saints that at least one major battle was fought somewhere in this region south of the Brosna between the men of Tara (Meath) and the men of Éile (Munster).[68] The distribution of well defended ringforts here seems to have been dictated by the strategic need of a border community.

Barrett examined ringfort settlement in the Dingle peninsula west of a line from Bulls Head to Brandon Creek.[69] This area consists of a number of flat low-lying alluvial areas (Ventry and Smerwick) divided by gently rounded hills and dominated by the mountain masses of Mount Eagle and Croaghmarhin in the west and Mount Brandon in the east.[70] Barrett identified 153 ringforts of which 74 could be classified; 31 were cashels (42% of surviving sites). Bivallate ringforts comprised 12% of the total, four of them located in one townland in the extreme south-east.[71] Ringforts avoided land below 30m and favoured land between 60m and 90m. As in Donegal, this is thought to reflect a need for better drainage and a finer view.[72] Barrett concluded that soil quality was a key determinant of settlement density. Brown earth and brown podzolic soils were favoured, and as these are widely distributed throughout Dingle, it accounts for the relatively even spread of ringforts there. However, one area of brown podzolic soil in the exposed west of the peninsula has a lower density than could be expected which suggests that climatic variables were also important to the ringfort builders.[73] The distribution of ecclesiastical sites corresponds broadly with that of ringforts with all such sites in the study area being located in areas of good soils.[74]

68 C. Plummer (ed. and trans.), *Bethada Náem nÉrenn* (2 vols, Oxford, 1922), see p. 104. For further information on county Offaly see M. Stout, 'Early Christian settlement, society and economy in Offaly' in W. Nolan and T.P. O'Neill (eds), *Offaly: History and society* (Dublin, 1998), pp 29–92. 69 Barrett, 'The ring-fort', fig. 7, p. 62. 70 Ibid., p. 218. 71 Ibid., table 3, p. 53, pp 64, 75, 77. 72 Ibid., table 18, pp 221–2. 73 Ibid., table 21, pp 227–31.

O'Flaherty examined Early Christian secular settlement in the north Kerry baronies of Iraghticonnor (0.88/km²) and Clanmaurice (1.oo/km²).[75] His study area of *c*.512/km² was divided into three regions: the first was Kerry Head, the most northerly ridge of the old red sandstone topography, which rises here to 210m, with a spine of high (61m) hills extending eastwards towards the estuary of the Cashen River. The lower, better drained slopes of this ridge have produced brown podzolic soils, whereas an extensive area of upland is covered in blanket bog; the south-eastern portion of O'Flaherty's study area is dominated by the Namurian shale upland known as the Stack's Mountains which rise to 356m. Gley soils and blanket peat predominate on this upland. Between the two aforementioned upland zones is a broad lowland Gust over 30m) stretching from Listowel to Ardfert. This lowland is floored, for the most part, with grey brown podzolic soils but gley soils are present in areas where the glacial till is poorly drained.[76]

O'Flaherty counted 480 ringfort sites in his study area to give a mean density of 0.94/km².[77] Few ringforts are located on Kerry Head, in the Stack's Mountains over 122m, or in the valley of the River Feale. The densest con centration of ringforts forms a band of sites below the 61m contour on the south-east-facing slopes of the sandstone ridge. Another area of notable density is found in the lowlands north and east of Ardfert. Most ringforts (395) in the study region are found below 61m in the limestone valleys, and altitudes over 122m are avoided.[78]

O'Flaherty examined the morphology and location of a random sample of 118 sites of which only 39 were sufficiently well preserved for study.[79] Despite the small sample, he noted that ringforts located on slopes averaged 31m in internal diameter and 37m in overall diameter, while ringforts on level ground averaged 36m internally and 49m in overall diameter; the steeper the slope, the smaller the diameter tended to be. In his own words, there is a 'tantalising hint that functional information may be obtained from site morphology'. He found no evidence that intervisibility between ringforts, or the lack of it, influenced ringfort size.[80] Ringforts in his study area do not show the preference for slopes that is observed so often elsewhere in Ireland, but minor topographical variations may still provide sloping locations for the large number of low-lying sites.

Prior to the completion of the Ordnance Survey 'Discovery' series of 1:50,000 maps (which have a 10m contour interval), the existing interval of 31m is not sufficient for assessing the topographical locations of ringforts from cartographic sources. As a result, ringfort which seem to be located in level terrain are, upon inspection, located in a rolling landscape. At Moyne in Tipperary, there is a rare

74 Ibid., fig. 24, p. 257.   **75** B. O'Flaherty, 'A locational analysis of the ringfort settlement of north county Kerry', unpublished MA thesis (University College Cork, 1982).   **76** Ibid., pp 65–72, 94–101.   **77** Ibid., p. 88.   **78** Ibid., p. 90.   **79** Ibid., pp 106–16.   **80** Ibid., p. 116–23, 132.

instance where an area has been re-surveyed with contour intervals of 1m. Here, ringforts are found in a fairly high concentration in an undulating topography which was not apparent from OS maps. Sites clearly avoid the tops of even the slightest hills, preferring a location on the break of slope which provided the best possible view and drainage given the nature of the landscape.[81]

ZONES OF VERY HIGH DENSITY

North-east Connaught has the highest density of ringforts in Ireland (1.52/km²). It comprises all of Sligo, north Roscommon and the baronies of Leitrim in north-west Leitrim and Gallen in north-east Mayo (fig. 14). The only significant gap in this dense distribution pattern is found above the 100m contour in the Ox Mountains, a ridge of Caledonian age and orientation which is composed of igneous and metamorphic rock. Blanket bog covers much of this upland and there is a considerable area to the north-east covered in low land blanket bog of Atlantic type. Elsewhere, where ringforts occur, they do so in abundance. The most significant coastal concentration in Ireland occurs in a *c*.5km wide band from Killala Bay, around Sligo Bay – along a narrow strip of degraded grey brown podzolic soils – continuing as far north as Mullaghmore Head. The coastal barony of Carbury, which includes the lime stone plateau of Ben Bulben and the rolling, gley-covered lowlands which lie below it, is at the northern limits of this ringfort grouping. The density of ringforts here is four times the national average (2.17/km²).

Inland from the coastal strip, massive concentrations of ringforts are grouped around drumlins. In Sligo these settlements took advantage of grey brown podzolic soils which formed on the well-drained hills between Ballymote, in the barony of Corran (1.82/km²) and Lough Arrow in Tirerrill barony (2.09/km²). Another concentration of ringforts stretches from the vicinity of Strokestown in north Roscommon – Roscommon barony reaches a density of 1.77/km² – to Ballinamore in Leitrim barony (1.31/km²) in southwest Leitrim. These sites are located mainly on gley soils although some better grey brown podzolic soils floor the area around Strokestown and Tulsk – including the royal/ritual site of Cruachain (plate 12). The valley of the Moy became another focus for secular settlement during the Early Christian period, especially in the Swinford/Killasser area in the barony of Gallen (1.72/km2) in Mayo. This grouping of sites takes advantage of a pocket of podzol soils formed on rolling, low-lying glacial till. An extension of this ringfort grouping, albeit at a lower density, extends into the hills, reaching altitudes of over

81 My thanks to Margaret Gowen for making this survey available to me.

Plate 12   Ringforts and associated field systems in Glenballythomas townland, Roscommon barony, just south of the royal site of Cruachain, Roscommon (CUCAP AVH 98).

100m between Tubbercurry and Collooney. Here, the ringfort occupants would have faced the obstacle of farming slightly wetter gley soils.

Although there is no clear reason as to why North-east Connaught was so densely settled, there being no spectacular agricultural or economic advantages existing in the region today, one very tentative possibility does present itself. Sligo boasts some of the largest groupings of pre-historic monuments in Ireland, most notably the passage tomb cemeteries at Carrowkeel and Carrowmore/Knocknarea. Although five millennia separate passage tombs from ringforts, it could be that the population explosion which occurred in the Early Christian period commenced in Sligo from an already substantial population baseline.

Farrelly examined a 37km² area on the eastern bank of the River Shannon in the barony of Leitrim, a drumlin area on a low-lying limestone base.[82] There are 102 definite ringforts in this densely settled region (2.76/km²) which is well above the mean density for North-east Connaught.[83] These have a tendency to avoid areas below 61m, preferring locations between 61m and 152m.[84] Most ringforts are located on gley soils which predominate in this study area. A pocket of well-drained rendzina soils attracted a cluster of six sites in Sheemore townland.[85] The mean distance to a ringfort's nearest neigh bour is 268m and no ringfort is over a kilometre distant from another site. In terms of land holding, this would have given an average of 32ha for each ring fort, slightly more than the 28ha holding attributed to the typical independent farmer of the Early Christian period (see below, chapter 7).[86] Seven of the ringforts are bivallate (6%). Their internal diameters are typical of those for Irish ringforts as a whole.[87]

Herity has published a detailed study of settlement features near the royal site of Cruachain in Roscommon.[88] Although his study area straddles four baronies in three zones - Roscommon in North-east Connaught; Ballymoe and Ballintober South in the high density area of South-east Connaught; and Castlereagh in the median density area of Central Mayo – it is discussed here because the highest concentration of ringforts in Herity's study area are in this zone of very high density. The study area of 107km² is underlain by limestone with a grey brown podzolic soil cover. To the north, the topography is dominated by the Rathcroghan plateau which rises to just under 150m. The southern portion of the study area is an undulating lowland with elevations of between *c*.60m–91m. This area is less well drained and contains a number of permanent lakes.[89] It is a region noted, even in Early Christian times, as one of the foremost pre-Christian centres of assembly, ritual activity and royal residence.[90]

Within this densely populated area (1 .25/km² on average rising to nine sites per square kilometre), only five ringforts are more than 1km distant from their nearest neighbour. Within ringfort groupings it is common for sites to be within 200m of one another. Ringforts are generally located on elevated or gently sloping ground, mainly in a narrow band of land at 300m below the Rathcroghan plateau, ensuring, even on the undulating ground, a good view in at least one direction.

82 Farrelly, 'Sample study', fig. 9, p. 17; fig. 10, p. 19; OS 1:10,560 sheet 27.   **83** Ibid., p. 5.   **84** Ibid., fig. 23, p. 53.   **85** Ibid., p. 57   **86** Ibid., p. 45, 67.   **87** Ibid., p. 25, figs 6–8, pp 12–4; fig. 11, p. 28; fig. 16, p. 33.   **88** M. Herity, 'A survey of the royal site of Cruachain in Connaught I: Introduction, the monuments and topography' in *Journal of the Royal Society of Antiquaries of Ireland*, cxiii (1983), pp 121–42; Herity, 'Cruachain III, pp 125–41; M. Herity, 'A survey of the royal site of Cruachain in Connaught IV: Ancient field systems at Rathcroghan and Carnfree' in *Journal of the Royal Society of Antiquaries of Ireland*, cxviii (1988), pp 67–84.   **89** Herity, 'Cruachain I', pp 122–3.   **90** Ibid., pp 124–5.

They are largely absent from the ridge tops and uplands dominated by ritual monuments and from low lying areas between 30m–61m which are, for the most part, poorly drained.[91] The ringfort builders also avoided exposed western slopes and in no instance is a ringfort sited in a hollow overlooked by higher ground.

Ringforts and Late Bronze Age/Iron Age ring barrows are shown by Herity to have complementary distributions, while early prehistoric burial mounds are found mainly in ringfort zones. This may not mean, as Herity has suggested, that ring barrows and ringforts are contemporary: a preference for slopes, as opposed to hilltops, is a commonly observed phenomenon in ring fort distributions. In addition, ecclesiastical sites in the area are located near 'ritual foci' in areas where ringforts are scarce.[92] Traditions involving such earlier monuments could have led to these sacred areas being avoided by Early Christian farmers and provided a natural setting for the new Christian ritual that replaced the old. Nonetheless, Herity has highlighted an important con sideration in distribution studies: non-economic issues can influence human decision making. Ultimately, the choice of location in Cruachain depended upon the influences of topography, earlier settlement patterns and population densities, and the relationships between individuals of varying status.

Keegan re-examined virtually the same region as above, an area of 80km² 3km distance containing 135 ringforts (1.70/km²) in the north and slightly west of the Cruachain study (fig. 27).[93] His analysis availed of the same statistical techniques applied to the same range of morphological, environmental and locational variables as used in the south-west midlands study (see above). The computerised classification procedure determined four ringfort types with some striking parallels to the earlier study. Six percent (12%, figures in brackets are the comparative values in the south-west midlands) of ringforts fell into a high-status category reminiscent of Cluster 2. These were bivallate ringforts built on impressive platforms but having internal diameters averaging only 31.14m (28.60m), smaller than the population mean for north Roscommon. But, like the comparable group in the south-west midlands, they had contrastingly large overall diameters of 56.62m (53.04m).[94] These are attributes associated with high status, 'royal compatible' ringforts throughout Ireland. Keegan identified another ringfort group with strong parallels to the small upland enclosures (Cluster 5) identified in the south-west midlands. These ringforts were only 27.05m (28.50m) in internal diameter on average and 37.12m (39.64) in overall diameter.[95] Unlike the south-west midlands however, they comprised a greater percentage of the ringfort population, 40% (23%) and were located in the lowest altitudes in the study area. The more typical ringforts in north Roscommon display morphological characteristics similar to south-west midlands' ringfort Clusters 1 and 3 but no ringfort cluster emerged which mirrored the very large and very well defended sites associated with territorial boundaries (cluster 4).

91 Herity, 'Cruachain III', pp 134–7, fig. 31.   92 Ibid., p. 141.   93 Keegan, 'Ringforts in north Roscommon', p. 6, figs 1, 8a.   94 Ibid., pp 28–9.   95 Ibid., pp 25–6.

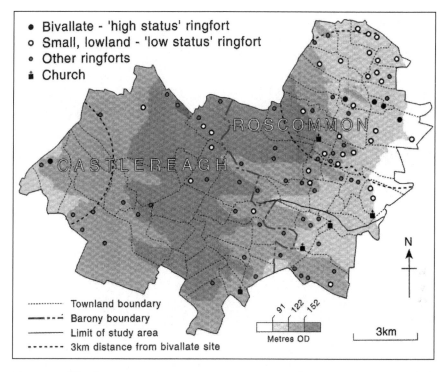

Figure 27   The distribution of ringforts immediately north of the royal site of Cruachain in Roscommon. Two-thirds of the smallest 'low-status' ringforts are found within 3km of bivallate, 'high-status' ringforts located mainly in the low-lying eastern portion of the study area. This distribution mirrors (in a lowland context) the juxtaposition of high- and low-status ringforts found in the south-west midlands (after Keegan, 1994).

The distribution of the different ringfort groupings also duplicates findings in the south-west midlands except that the high status/low status ringfort associations are found in a low-lying situation in Roscommon rather than in an upland setting. Most of the high status sites are found in the north-east of the study area and two-thirds of the low status sites are found within 3km of these – as opposed to one-fifth of ringforts from the other two clusters representing more typical ringforts.

West Clare is a zone of very high ringfort density (1.16/km²) comprising west Clare and two baronies in south Galway on Galway Bay (fig. 14). This overall high density is maintained despite large tracts of territory within the area which lack settlement. The largest such zone without ringforts is the bog-covered upland formed on Namurian shales centred on Slievecallan and Ben Dash. The low-lying karst on the Clare/Galway border is also thinly settled. The main concentration of ringforts is found in a band stretching from the bare

Plate 13   Ringforts and field systems in Ballybaun townland, barony of Corcomroe in the
karst landscape east of Kilfenora, Clare. Dense ringfort settlement continues
onto grasslands to the south and north-west of the Burren (CUCAP BGJ 6).

limestone pavements of the Burren ($1.70/km^2$) at Ballyvaughan to the shallow limestone drift-covered small hills north of Ennis (plate 13). At this point the band of dense settlement bifurcates: one band of ringforts continues along the lime stone drift east of the Fergus river, from Quin, in the barony of Bunratty Upper ($1.62/km^2$) to the Shannon estuary while the other stretches across the east-facing hills west of the Fergus to an area of poorly drained gley soils formed on Namurian shale deposits. A narrow band of ringforts extends from the main Burren concentration westwards across the south-facing slopes formed of Namurian shale between Kilfenora and Hags Head. Ringforts are also plentiful on the Fanore coast in the Burren and on Loop Head. Finally, a pocket of dense ringfort settlement exists on the shallow brown earth soils of the lowlands south of the Dunkellin river, west and south of Galway bay.

One study of the Burren region notes how townland boundaries bore some relationship to secular settlement, suggesting an Early Christian origin for these boundaries.[96] 60% of ringforts were located within 61m of a townland boundary, which accounts for no more than 40% of the total land area. All ecclesiastical sites fall within this 61m wide boundary zone. Despite claims to the contrary, this is the only area in Ireland where a real relationship exists between ringforts and townland boundaries beyond what would be expected from a random point sample. In the south-west midlands, north Roscommon and in Antrim north of Lough Neagh, ringforts showed no bias towards townland boundary locations.[97]

West Limerick continues the band of high ringfort density south of the Shannon estuary in Limerick (fig. 23). This region, with an overall ringfort density of $1.52/km^2$, is the western limit of the Golden Vale and is bounded on the south and west by poorly drained gley soils found on Namurian shale deposits at heights of over 150m. The Maigue river forms the area's eastern boundary although there is still a very high settlement density to the east of it; Pubblebrien barony, at the extreme east of this region, has a ringfort density of $1.21/km^2$, which then reduces (relatively speaking) as one moves eastwards into **North Munster**. The main concentration of ringforts in **West Limerick** is found along the eastern boundaries of Shanid and Glenquin baronies in a narrow band which coincides precisely with a ring of lower Visean limestone, overlain with better drained grey brown podzolic soils. The concentration of ringforts is divided by barony boundaries which reduces the impact of this zone statistically. However, Connello Lower, which is slightly east of the main concentration in an area of shallow brown earth soils, has a very high density of $1.98/km^2$.

96 M. Hennessy, 'Territorial organisation in the barony of Burren, county Clare', unpublished BA thesis (University College Dublin, 1981), see p. 28.   97 M. Stout, 'Ringforts', pp. 210–12, fig. 5b; Keegan, 'Ringforts in north Roscommon', p. 15; McErlean, 'Early Christian settlement pattern and structure', p. 32.

RINGFORTS AND ECCLESIASTICAL SITES

Although the distribution of ecclesiastical sites is outside the scope of this study, some research has addressed the relationship between ringforts and ecclesiastical sites. It is not yet possible to compare both distributions at a national level. While ringforts can be identified with a high degree of certainty from cartographic and aerial photographic sources, ecclesiastical sites can not, as the presence of a church on a map provides no indication of its date. Historical sources which might provide a valid impression of overall distribution patterns, grossly underestimate the number of Early Christian establishments. Swan has shown that intense field work can treble the number of known early ecclesiastical sites.[98] In Westmeath, 29 early churches were recorded by Gwynn, *et al.*,[99] but 66 more were identified after a closer examination of all ecclesiastical sites in the county. Swan's provisional national map of ecclesiastical enclosures, does, however, point towards a dichotomy in secular and ecclesiastical distributions. Ecclesiastical enclosures, like ringforts, are found throughout Ireland, but they occur most frequently in a wide band across the midlands, north of a line between Dublin Bay and the Shannon estuary and south of a line from Dundalk Bay to Clew Bay (fig. 28). In Sligo, the area of densest ringfort settlement, ecclesiastical enclosures are rare. The types of location favoured by both types of settlement differ. Ecclesiastical sites tend to have a low-lying riverine distribution – seldom occurring over 120m and almost never above 180m – which is also at odds with the distribution of ringforts.[100] One study establishes a tentative link between religious establishments and the secular population within ringforts that would have patronised the ecclesiastical sites.[101] There is a close statistical correlation between the number of ringforts and ecclesiastical sites in the eight Dublin baronies as both ringfort and church numbers decline from south to north.[102] Nonetheless, the upland/lowland dichotomy was still present, a point well illustrated by the barony of Rathdown where ringforts were found almost exclusively above the 182m contour and ecclesiastical sites considerably lower.[103] As noted above, a similarly complementary distribution was observed north of Lough Neagh in the baronies of Toome Upper and Toome Lower (fig. 17) and in Morgallion barony in Meath (fig. 21). All but one of thirty church sites in the

---

98 L. Swan, 'The Early Christian ecclesiastical sites of county Westmeath' in J. Bradley (ed.), *Settlement and society in Medieval Ireland; Studies presented to F.X. Martin* (Kilkenny, 1988), pp 3–32. Swan also notes that half the existing parishes have one early church site which suggests that parish boundaries have their origins in the Early Christian period.   **99** Ordnance Survey, *Monastic Ireland* (second ed., Dublin, 1979).   **100** L. Swan, 'Enclosed ecclesiastical sites and their relevance to settlement patterns of the first millennium A.D.' in Reeves-Smyth and Hamond (eds), *Landscape archaeology*, pp 269–94, see p. 273.   **101** G. Stout and M. Stout, 'Patterns in the past', pp 5–25.   **102** Ibid., fig. 3, p. 17. This relationship existed before and after the contribution of aerial photography was taken into account.   **103** Ibid., fig. 2, p. 14.

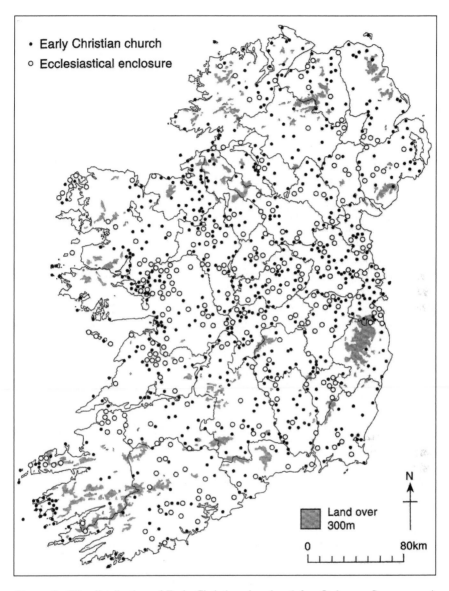

Figure 28   The distribution of Early Christian churches (after Ordnance Survey, 1979) and ecclesiastical enclosures (after Swan, 1983; see Stout and Stout 2011, p. 51 for an up-to-date version of this map). For a more detailed discussion of the distribution of ecclesiastical sites see M. Stout, 2012.

Antrim study area were on the periphery of, or in isolation from main ringfort groupings. South of the drumlin belt in the low-lying area of Morgallion, only 10% of ringforts were found in contrast to 86% of church sites. There is, however, an important exception in the case of the Early Christian site at Nobberbeg in Morgallion which was located just south of a trivallate ringfort.

In Offaly, the mean altitude of ecclesiastical centres (78m) is 20m below the mean for ringforts (98m), a significant difference taking into consideration of ecclesiastical sites (in the Brosna valley) is not mirrored in the main areas of ringfort concentration (in the extreme north-west and south-west of the county). A detailed study of an area in the south of Garrycastle barony illustrates this inverse relationship (fig. 29). This is low-lying terrain with extensive tracts of raised bog. The productive land, mainly grey brown podzolic soils, occur in regions above the 91m contour and along the River Brosna. There are six Early Christian ecclesiastical sites in this 70km2 study area, all within 2km of the Brosna whose well drained valley forms a pass through bogland lying on either side. In contrast, secular settlement within ringforts was located on higher, better drained ground which is aligned along a northeast/south-west axis north of the Brosna. Unlike ecclesiastical sites, ringforts in general and high status bivallate sites in particular are removed as far as possible from two probable arteries of communication; the Brosna in the south and the *Escir Riada* to the north. However, some large, well defended ringforts, similar to strategically located cluster 4 ringforts identified in the southwest midlands, are located near both ecclesiastical sites and routeways.

There is a contradictory distribution pattern to the upland/lowland dichotomy described above. The Clogher area features a royal ringfort and an ecclesiastical site which formed the core of the dioceses of the same name established at the synod of Ráith Bressail in 1111 and it was presumably a centre for both church and state long before that date.[104] A similar juxtaposition occurs in Offaly. In a 70km² well settled (0.60/km2) area in the south-west of the county, the ecclesiastical enclosure of Seir Kieran is located at some remove from most ringforts (fig. 30). The exception is the now sadly destroyed trivallate ringfort at Oakleypark townland, located just upslope from the ecclesiastical centre and on or near the probable course of the main north/south corridor through the midlands (plate 14). These two sites formed the core of a parish which was a detached portion of the Leinster diocese of Ossory within a Munster diocese on the border of Meath; clearly it was a very strategic and isolated position requiring the defensive measures afforded by the trivallate ringfort. The relationship is similar to the case of Nobberbeg in Morgallion

---

104 F. Byrne, 'Dioceses as defined at the synod of Ráith Bressail 1111' in T. Moody, F. Martin and F. Byrne (eds), *A new history of Ireland; vol. ix, maps, genealogies, lists; a companion to Irish history part ii* (Oxford, 1984), map 24, pp 26, 101.

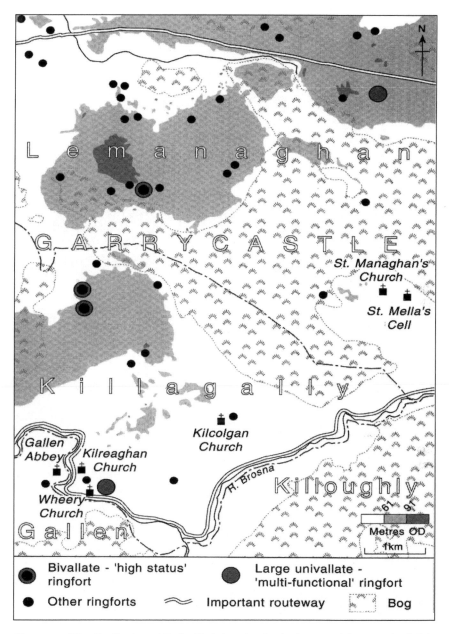

Bivallate - 'high status' ringfort

Large univallate - 'multi-functional' ringfort

Other ringforts

Important routeway

Bog

Figure 29   The distribution of Early Christian sites in the barony of Garrycastle, Offaly
highlights the relationship between lay and ecclesiastical elements of society.
Ringforts occupy the better drained hill slopes, with church sites located in
the river valleys near important arteries of communication. The 'high-status'
ringforts are at some distance from both roadways and church sites. Large
'multi-functional' ringforts are in strategic locations.

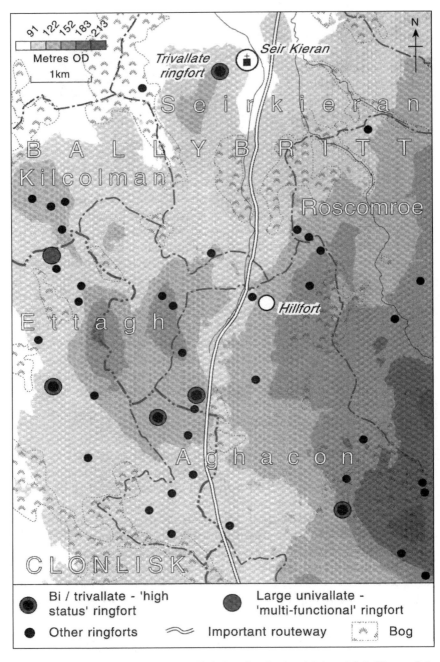

Figure 30   The distribution of Early Christian sites in the vicinity of Seir Kieran, Seir
Kieran was an island parish belonging to the Leinster diocese of Ossory within
a Munster diocese on the border with Meath. The ecclesiastical enclosure and
trivallate ringfort are separated from an even spread of ring forts by a *c.*2.5km
wide 'buffer zone'.

Plate 14   The large monastic enclosure of Seir Kieran is overlooked by a trivallate ringfort at Oakleypark townland in the barony of Ballybritt, Offaly (CUCAP AYN 46)

SUMMARY OF DISTRIBUTION

It is difficult to encapsulate the distribution of ringforts throughout Ireland, when, as we have seen, there are wide variations even within areas of similar overall density. Nonetheless, some generalisation can be made. At the most basic level, ringforts are not found in areas which cannot support farming communities. Accepting that ringforts were primarily constructed as a defence against cattle raids, McCormick believes that below a certain threshold of human and cattle density cattle raiding was not 'cost-effective', and no ringforts were constructed. Thus the distribution of ringforts becomes an index of Early Christian stocking rates.[105] Throughout Ireland where ringforts are found, they usually display a preference for sloping or hilly terrain. This preference has been recognised since the beginning of modern ringfort studies when Westropp observed:

> The selection [of a sloping site for a fort], apart from the question of drainage, may have arisen from a wish to secure a situation at once lifted above the mists of the plain, and yet sheltered from some prevailing wind, which would have been violent on the more level summit. Strange to say, however, the garth is not as a rule 'terraced-up' to a level.[106]

Davies believed that hilltop ringforts occurred south of a line from Newry, Armagh, Maghery, Carnteel, Carrickmore, Clogher, and Clones. North of this line ringforts are located on hill slopes or along river valleys.[107] The hilltop siting has not received further confirmation, while a desire for a location on sloping ground is affirmed in the huge number of ringforts in the drumlin belt – where they are usually located on the brow of individual drumlins – and on valley sides – from the eastern slopes of the Sperrin mountains, to the undulating kame topography of the north midlands, and the south-facing slopes of the ridge and valley province, especially in the Lee valley. Areas of more level, low-lying terrain are normally regions of low ringfort density, and this is irrefutable if the distribution in Leinster is real and not merely the result of post-Anglo-Norman destruction rates. Some exceptions to this rule do exist, however, most notably the high concentration of ringforts on the eastern shores of Lough Neagh and the broad lowland between Listowel and Ardfert in Kerry. Yet, as was seen in the low-lying area near Moyne in Tipperary, the builders of ringforts took advantage of even the slightest undulations in local topography to provide a sloping site for their farmsteads.

---

105 F. McCormick, 'Cows, ringforts and the origins of Early Christian Ireland' in *Emania*, xiii (1995), pp 33–7.   **106** Westropp, 'Ancient forts of Ireland', p. 680.   **107** O. Davies, 'Appendix' in E. Watson, 'Prehistoric sites in south Antrim' in *Ulster Journal of Archaeology*, iii (1940), p. 151.

By and large, it is also true to say that ringforts, meeting as they did the needs of a cattle rearing population, were located in areas of good quality soils and thus had a distribution broadly similar to contemporary dispersed farming patterns. Evans, when describing the distribution of ringforts in the six counties, noted that the vast majority were found below the 152m contour, a distribution with a 'strikingly 'modern' appearance'.[108] In Down, all ringforts lay below the high water mark of cultivation reached in the nineteenth century and many modern farms were located near or within ringforts.[109] The upper limit of ringforts changes according to environmental conditions, however, and farms on the glacial deposits in the south-west midlands found advantageous locations at altitudes near 300m. In choosing sloping locations, ringfort builders avoided the heaviest lowland clays, preferring instead glacial sands and gravels.[110] The logical avoidance of peatlands is another constant of ringfort distributions. But an economy which emphasised cattle rearing was not con strained to the highest quality soil types. Many ringforts are found on poorly drained gley soils, especially in north Munster and Connaught. Because of their poor drainage and heavy, silty texture, gley soils are not suitable to tillage, but they can be suitable for livestock. If grazing is properly managed so as to prevent poaching and rush infestation, pastures on gley soils could probably support one cow per hectare.[111] In poorly drained drumlin zones and on wetter upper slopes, gley soils were tolerated; soil quality was traded off against other locational advantages and strategic needs.

Throughout much of Ireland, regardless of overall settlement density, ringforts are not evenly spread across the landscape even when topographical conditions permitted this. Thus, in areas of mean density, square kilometres containing four ringforts are not unusual, and in areas of high density groups of up to nine ring forts are known. Proudfoot, and others, have attributed this clustering of sites to a pioneering movement into wooded areas, in which case groupings represent innumerable cultivated islands in a sea of forest.[112] Another view, that the structure of society and not environmental constraints dictated ringfort distribution is dis cussed below. This grouping of ringforts may not, however, apply to the drumlin zone where the 'basket of eggs' topography often imposed a scattered distribution of sites.[113] One ringfort per drumlin was common in Down,[114] although this was not the case in that part of the drumlin zone in Leitrim examined by Farrelly.

Everywhere in Ireland a hierarchy of ringforts has been noted with the percentage of 'high-status' bivallate ringforts remaining fairly constant. In the few areas where

108 E. Evans and M. Gaffikin, 'Belfast Naturalist's Field Club survey of antiquities: megaliths and raths' in *Irish Naturalist's Journal*, v (1935), pp 242–52, see pp 244, 250–1, fig. 2. 109 Proudfoot, 'Settlement and economy in county Down', pp 447–9. 110 Evans and Gaffikin, 'Megaliths and raths', pp 244, 250–1, fig. 2. 111 T. Finch and P. Ryan, *Soils of county Limerick* (Dublin, 1966), see p.104. 112 Proudfoot, 'Settlement and economy in county Down', p. 458. 113 Evans and Gaffikin, 'Megaliths and raths', pp 244, 250–1, fig. 2. 114 Proudfoot, 'Settlement and economy in county Down', p. 449.

ringforts morphology has been examined in relation to topography and other locational factors, the distribution pattern tentatively suggests that this hierarchy may be attributed to one roughly similar settlement model. In north Kerry and the south-west midlands, ringforts tended to be smaller at higher attitudes; the reverse of this was the case in Roscommon. But in both of the latter study areas the least significant ringforts were found in association with the most impressive sites, while more typical ringforts were more evenly (independently) distributed.

Common too is the complementary distribution of ringforts and ecclesiastical sites. At a small scale this is reflected in the upland/lowland settlement dichotomy demonstrated by the high density of ecclesiastical enclosures throughout the midlands, an area of low ringfort density, and in more detailed studies of both secular and ecclesiastical settlement in Dublin and Offaly. At a larger scale, church sites are often shown to be located at the margins of ringfort groupings; this is the case in the Brosna valley, Cruachain, Morgallion and north of Lough Neagh. Where exceptions to this church/secular dichotomy occur – as in the cases of Nobberbeg, Seir Kieran and Clogher – equally exceptional political and territorial factors seem to be the primary influence. And, as the group of high-status, well defended ringforts in the marchlands of Offaly suggest, disputed territorial boundaries may have also created exceptions to the common distribution pattern of ringforts.

Not all of the characteristics of ringfort distribution can be so readily explained, however, and one of the chief problem lies in the variation of settlement density in areas which do not seem to have greatly different environ mental conditions. Climatic variables which would have favoured grass growth do not correlate with the distribution of ringforts,[115] although conditions more favourable to grass growth in Ireland as a whole could explain why the dominant pastoral economy developed here but was not replicated else where in Europe. Further, I do not feel that variations in ringfort densities are adequately explained by post-Early Christian settlement patterns. *All* of the Anglo-Norman tillage areas in Ireland do not have low ringfort densities. Westmeath, Tipperary and Kilkenny present a serious challenge to interpretations that this settlement pattern is based on medieval and subsequent destruction rates. Even if we leave aside the problem of Leinster, what, for instance, can explain the very high density of ringforts in Sligo? Why is the east of the Golden Vale less densely populated than the west? What advantages did the drumlin topography of east Cavan/south Monaghan have over the drumlins of the Erne valley? What can explain high densities in west Clare and in Antrim east of Lough Neagh? A large pre-Christian population base might go some way to explaining densities in Sligo and west Clare but many of the answers

---

115 Meteorological services, Dublin, 'Air frost and growing season' in Royal Irish Academy, *Atlas of Ireland*, p. 31.

may lie in aspects of the Early Christian landscape that the modern geographer cannot assess, like the extent of forest cover or regions of political turmoil where farming enterprises were discouraged. Also, the population estimated at half a million persons might not have given rise to land scarcity, permitting Early Christian farmers to inhabit areas which they saw as being more advantageous. Contemporary perceptual advantages, like proximity to a just king (or a good story teller), or what Early Christians regarded as a fine view, cannot be easily gleaned from the modern landscape.

7 Early Christian settlement and society

If no ringforts had survived in Ireland it would still be possible to reconstruct this settlement form from contemporary sources, and more importantly, the society which built them. Writings from the period, especially Early Irish law, describe ringfort morphology, function and economy, their distribution and relationship with ecclesiastical settlement. Other sources, which may have their origins in the Early Christian period but were written down at a later date, also shed light on the society which lived within ringforts. As it is, ringforts do survive, and from excavation and analysis of distribution we can tell a great deal about the society that built them. Written sources and physical remains combine to permit convincing models of seventh to ninth-century Irish society. Early Christian settlement was organised within a network of petty kingdoms. There were at any one time at least 150 territorial units, known as *túatha*, each containing perhaps 3,000 men women and children.[1] The *túath* is roughly equivalent with modem baronies.[2] All examinations of ringfort morphology reveal a hierarchy of sites, mirroring the hierarchical nature of early Irish society which dwelt within these territorial units. Eleven legal tracts describe social hierarchies with various degrees of sub-division and complexity.[3] McLeod maintains that many of the contradictions between tracts are ascribable to transcription errors or merely elaborations of one basic legal system which applied throughout Ireland. While this may oversimplify matters, his synthesis provides a clear summary of quite complicated Early Irish laws of status (table 4). Most simply, the laws describe a society in which there were two significant groups: kings and lords; and commons or free farmers. Members of each rank had a specified amount of land, number of clients and an honour price that was paid to an individual for any major offence committed against him.[4]

1 F. Kelly, *A guide to early Irish law* (Dublin, 1988), see pp 3–4   2 D. Binchy (ed.), *Críth Gablach* (Dublin, 1941), see p. 109.   3 N. McLeod, 'Interpreting Early Irish law: status and currency (part 1)' in *Zeitschrift fur Celtische Philologie*, xli (1986), pp 46–65; N. McLeod, 'Interpreting Early Irish law: status and currency (part 2)' in *Zeitschrift fur Celtische Philologie*, xiii (1987), pp 41–115. See part 1, table 1, pp 52–3.   4 Kelly, *Early Irish law*, p. 8.

Table 4
Summary of free status, land holding and clientship from the law tracts

Grade	English translation	Honour price (in cumal)	Tír cumaile	Hectares	Number of bóaire clients	Number of ócaire clients
Rí túaithe	King of territory	7.0	7	97.3	—	—
Aire forgill	Lord of superior testimony	5.0	6	83.4	5	6
Aire ard	High lord	3.3	5	69.5	4	5
Aire túise	Lord of leadership	2.5	4	55.6	2	3
Aire déso	Lord	1.7	3	41.7		
Bóaire	Cow lord	0.8	2	27.8	—	—
Ócaire	Young lord	0.5	1	13.9	—	—

At the pinnacle of a *túath* is the rí or king. According to a poem which accompanies *Críth Gablach*, an Irish law tract dating to *c.*AD700, a king had a solid grounding in the minutiae of land measurement and division which ultimately determined settlement characteristics:

Madbé ríg rofessir	If you are a king you should know
recht flatha	the prerogative of a ruler,
fothoth iar mbiad	reflection according to rank,
mescbaid a slógh	contention in the host (?)
sabaid cuirmmtigi	cudgels in the ale-house,
cuir mesca	contracts made in drunkenness,
mess tíri	valuation of lands
tomus forrag	measurement by poles,
forberta diri	augmentation of penalty,
díthle mesraid	theft of tree-fruit,[5]
mórmúin mrugrechta	the great wealth of farm-law,
mrogad coicrích	marking of common bounds,
cor cuálne	planting of stakes,
córus rinde	regulation of points,
rann etir comorbbe	sharing among joint heirs,
comaithig do garmmaimm	naming joint husbandmen ...[6]

A king was also required to know what fines to levy for damage to enclosures, woodland and roads and penalties for theft. Judge, farmer, surveyor; the ascendancy of domestic and legal ability over martial duties for kingship in the early seventh century is manifest in this poem.

Below *rí túath* were approximately four divisions of aire, or lords, of varying status.[7] The *aire forgill* was a class of noble whose status was based on being formerly royal or having a strong family relationship to royalty.[8] This noble grade and the *aire ard* had military functions and could offer defaulting debtors sanctuary within their

5 Ibid., pp 356–7.   6 E. MacNeill, 'Ancient Irish law: law of status and franchise' in *Proceedings of the Royal Irish Academy*, xxxvi (1923), pp 265–316, see p. 308.   7 McLeod, 'Interpreting Early Irish law (part 1)', pp 57–65.   8 McLeod, 'Interpreting Early Irish law (part 2)', p. 52

ringforts.[9] The size of their land-holdings is indicated in a law tract which states that the lowest grade of freeman, the *ócaire*, 'possesses a *tír cumaile* of land (13.9ha) and every grade from that up to *rí túath* has respectively a *tír cumaile* of land in excess over each preceding one'.[10] Therefore, the noble grades held between 41.4ha and 97.3ha of land.[11] It is possible that in reality the legally defined *tír cumaile* of 13.9ha would have had its size based on the ability to support cattle and was, as a result, larger in poorer pastureland.

In my interpretation of these legal sources, a proportion of the noble land holdings would have been 'let' to *ócaire* clients. Noble status is thus indicated in an indirect way in that all the land of the *aire forgill* and the *aire ard* was allotted to *ócaire* clients. In contrast, an *aire túise* seems to have farmed one-quarter of his land, with an *aire déso* being directly involved in agricultural production on two-thirds of his property.[12]

Of the non-noble grades, the *bóaire* was the lowest grade of freeman, a small independent farmer who held *c.*27.8ha of land in his own right. The *ócaire* was the lowest grade of freeman, and was distinguished by having no land of his own. He would have leased a tir cumaile (13.9ha) of land from a lord on a yearly basis for the payment of one cow, in addition to the customary advance of cattle:

> He has seven *cumals* of land. It is that [which is] a cow's land in Irish law; it sustains seven cows for a year, i.e. seven cows are driven into it [and] he leaves the seventh cow on the [last] day of the year in rent for the land.[13]

The hierarchy intuitively suggests a correlation between these free grades of society and ringforts which display a similar hierarchy. Confirmation of this link is found in *Críth Gablach*, the best contemporary source for ringfort morphology.[14] MacNeill translates the relevant passage as follows:

---

9 Ibid., pp 43–6.   10 *Ancient laws of Ireland*, vol. ii (Dublin, 1869), see p. 13.   11 According to MacNeill, 'Ancient Irish law', pp. 286–7, the basic unit of land holding in the Early Christian period was the *tír cumaile* which measured six *forrach* by twelve *forrach*. The *forrach* was equal to twelve *fertach*, the *fertach* being a loan word from the Latin word for perch (*pertica*) which was twelve feet long (3.66m). A *tír cumaile* equalled 13.9ha [(3.66 x 12 x 6) x (3.66 x 12 x 12)]. It cannot be taken for granted that the *fertach*, on which all of the other linear and areal measurements are based, was exactly twelve modem feet. It should be home in mind, therefore, that while measurements in given in tenths of hectares they are only the metric equivalents of imperial approximations. See also Kelly, *Early Irish law*, p. 99.   12 N. Patterson, in pers. comm., disagrees with my suggestion that *ócaire* holdings came from land associated with lords and lordly rank. She gives three reasons for this view: *Críth Gablach* implies that renting land was a bad practice; other tribal lands could have been used, heirless land for example, and in such a sparsely populated society those without access to land would be few.   13 McLeod, 'Interpreting Early Irish law (part 2)', p. 61. The seven *cumal* mentioned here is approximately one *tír cumaile*.   14 T. Charles-Edwards, '*Críth Gablach* and the law of status' in *Peritia*, v (1986), pp 53–73, see p. 53. *Críth Gablach* is an Irish law tract dating to *c.*700 AD which describes the determinants of social status, one of the chief concerns of contemporary jurists.

What is the due of a king who is always in residence at the head of his tuath? Seven score feet [42.56m] of perfect feet are the measure of his stockade on every side. Seven feet [2.13m] are the thickness of its earth work, and twelve feet [3.65m] its depth. It is then that he is a king, when ramparts of vassalage surround him. What is the rampart of vassalage? Twelve feet [3.65m] are the breadth of its opening and its depth and it measure towards the stockade. Thirty feet [9.12m] are its measure outwardly.[15]

These measurements are consistent with field-based findings. 'On every side' suggests circularity; a tendency towards circularity is observed in most enclosures. The internal diameter of a king's ringfort, 42.56m, exceeds the mean for ringforts as a whole (*c*.30m); approximately 18% of ringforts in Rathcroghan match or exceed this figure, 12% in the south-west midlands, 11% in Monaghan, 6% in parts of Leitrim, 5% in Donegal.[16] In Early Irish law, base clients (*giállnae*) of a king or of any higher rank owed a fixed amount of manual labour to their superiors, including help in the construction of their lord's ringfort.[17] It follows from this that the more base clients owing labour service to a noble, the greater will be the size of that noble's earthwork. Thus, the ramparts of vassalage referred to in *Críth Gablach* are the earthworks erected as part payment of the labour requirements of a king's base clients. They refer to bivallate ringforts having 9.12m wide defences and an overall diameter – assuming the internal diameter is the same – of 60.80m. Once again, this exceeds the mean for ringforts as a whole (*c*.45m); approximately 16% of ringforts in Rathcroghan have overall diameters greater than 60m, 15% in the south-west midlands, 6% in parts of Leitrim.[18] And as was noted above, bivallate sites themselves constitute approximately 18% of the ringfort population.

Analysis of the morphological characteristics of the five ringfort classes in the south-west midlands highlights further similarities with the law tracts. The 'multi-functional, strategically located' cluster 4 ringforts had the highest circularity index (.91), had an average internal diameter of 46.97m and average overall diameter of 67.63m (as opposed to 42.56m and 60.80m, respectively, in the laws). The overall width of the ramparts of vassalage of 9.12m is remarkably close to 10.33m, the mean width of the defences for cluster 4 ringforts. Cluster 2 ringforts had defences averaging 12.22m in width, exceeding the 'norm' for the ringfort associated with *rí túaithe*, further emphasising the 'high status' nature of that ringfort class. Ringfort clusters 1, 3 and 5 have mean defence widths of only *c*.6m.[19] No mention is made of the ringforts belonging to the lower grades in the law tracts, but as the description of a high status ringfort conforms to, at most,

15 MacNeill, 'Ancient Irish law', p. 305. **16** Herity, 'Cruachain III', fig. 296, p, 131; M. Stout, 'Ringforts', fig. 4a, p. 209; Farrelly, 'A sample study', figs 11–2, pp 28–9. **17** Kelly, *Early Irish law*, p. 30. **18** Herity, 'Cruachain III', fig, 296, p, 131; M. Stout, 'Ringforts', fig. 4a, p. 209; Farrelly, 'A sample study', figs 11–12, pp 28–9. **19** M. Stout, 'Ringforts', pp 232–4.

the largest one-fifth of sites, it is logical to assume that the smaller ringforts were occupied by the lower grades.[20] The large group of 'typical' cluster 3 ringforts in the south-west midlands probably housed *bóaire*, the small, independent farmers. It also seems reasonable to suggest that the resources of time and labour spent on building an enclosure on rented land would be a good deal less than those expended on one's own property. This likelihood is supported by a reference to the *ócaire* dwellings in which the members of this class were said to have had a smaller honour price 'because the hospitality of his house is not complete and because he is not capable of undertaking surety ... because of the smallness of his means'.[21] Thus the smallest ringforts in the south-west midlands must be linked to the *ócaire* grades.[22]

Another contemporary description of a ringfort comes from 'Aisling Meic Conglinne' a poem which, although dating from the eleventh century, describes eighth-century persons and events including the battle of Allen in 722.[23] In this satire, the protagonist makes a dream visit to a ringfort made of food:

Coem in dúnad rancahmár	The fort we reached was beautiful
cona rathaib robrechtán	With works of custards thick,
resin loch anall:	Beyond the loch.
ba himm úr a erdrochat,	New butter was the bridge in front,
a chaisel ba gelchraithnecht	The rubble dyke was wheaten white,
a shondach ba sáll.	Bacon the palisade.
Ba suairc segda a shuidiugud	Stately, pleasantly it sat,
in tige treoin trebarda,	A compact house and strong.
in n-dechad iartain:	Then I went in:
a chomla do thirmcharnu,	The door of it was dry meat,
a thairsech do thurarán,	The threshold was bare bread,
do maethluib a fraig.	Cheese-curds the sides.[24]

This description highlights some key morphological points; the ringfort in the poem is defended by a fosse across which it was necessary to build a bridge; this fosse was outside of a stone bank, and the top of the bank was defended by a palisade.

---

20 Mytum disagrees, believing that ringforts were occupied only by the upper echelons of society; in my view, this conclusion is incompatible with excavation results and contemporary sources. His opinion is founded on the small number of sites occupied at any one time (10,000 by his calculations) and the lack of archaeological evidence for grain stores which is, in turn, evidence for the receipt of grain as tribute from the lower orders of society. The figure of 10,000 is based on the assumption that each of the 60,000 ringforts (Mytum's estimation) was occupied for a 100-year period and that occupation within ringforts spanned a 600-year period. See Mytum, *Origins*, pp 131–2, 152–5. **21** McLeod, 'Interpreting early Irish law (part 2)', p. 71. **22** M. Stout, 'Ringforts', p. 235. **23** P. Ní Chatháin in a lecture to the Royal Society of Antiquaries of Ireland, 1992. **24** K. Meyer (ed. and trans.) *Aisling Meic Conglinne, The vision of Mac Conglinne*, second edition (New York, 1974), see p. 36.

The latter point is a characteristic of ringforts challenged (wrongly in my view) by Mallory and MacNeill (see above, chapter 1).

The Early Christian dating of ringforts is further confirmed in written sources, in exactly contemporary references to these enclosures in Early Irish law, and in the lives of the saints by simply forming the backdrop to much of the activity which takes place. The long-term occupation of ringforts is also seen in the beautiful eighth-century poem which contrasts ephemeral human life with the enduring occupation of ringforts; in this case the large platform ringfort outside Rathangan, Kildare (plate 15), from AD579 to well after AD652:

Ind ráith i comair in dairfedo,	The fort opposite the oakwood
ba Bruidgi, ba Cathail,	Once it was Bruidge's, it was Cathal's,
ba hÁedo, ba hÁilello,	It was Aed's, it was Ailill's,
ba Conaing, ba Cuilíni	It was Conaing's, it was Cuiline's
ocus ba Máele Dúin.	And it was Maelduin's—
Ind ráith d'éis each ríg ar úair,	The fort remains after each in his turn,
ocus int shlúaig foait i n-úir.	And the kings asleep in the ground.[25]

While there is no indication of the pre-Norman demise of this settlement type as demonstrated by scientific dating, there are definite indications that they were not occupied from Norman times. In the *Topography of Ireland*, Giraldus Cambrensis misunderstood the origin of ringforts due to their long abandonment;

But in [838] the Norwegians put in at the Irish shores with a great fleet. Their leader, who was called Turgesius, quickly subjected the whole island to himself in many varied conflicts and fierce wars. He journeyed throughout the whole country and strengthened it with strong forts in suitable places.

And so to this day, as remains and traces of ancient times, you will find here many trenches, very high and round and often in groups of three, one outside of the other, as well as walled forts which are still standing, although now empty and abandoned. For the people of Ireland have no use for castles. Woods are their forts and swamps are their trenches.[26]

The oft-quoted thirteenth-century reference to the construction by the O'Briens of 'a princely circular abode of earth' probably refers to the construction of a motte by a Gaelic chieftain rather than the continued construction of ringforts in the medieval period. And an early fourteenth-century reference to 'Ruan of the grass-topped hollow cahers' confirms the abandonment of ringforts in the medieval

25 G. Murphy (ed. and trans.), *Early Irish Lyrics; eighth to twelfth century* (Oxford, 1956), p. xvi. Also quoted in M. de Paor and L. de Paor, *Early Christian Ireland*, p. 80. **26** J. Ó Meara (trans.), *The history and topography of Ireland* (London, 1982), see pp 118–19. My thanks to Katharine Simms for help with these medieval sources.

Plate 15   'The fort opposite the oakwood' near the village of Rathangan, in the barony
of Offaly East, Kildare is one of the few ringforts that can be dated from
historical sources.

period.[27] However, some ringforts remained occupied, or were reoccupied at a later
date. The sixteenth-century Ua Duibhdabhoirenn law-school was housed within
Cahermacnaghten, a large stone-built ringfort in the Burren, Clare which boasts a
two-storeyed, late-medieval gateway.[28] An enclosure in Ballinacor, Wicklow seems
to have been refortified in 1596,[29] and Bartlett's early seventeenth-century maps
of Ulster clearly show thatched cabins within ringforts.[30] This continuity of use,
however, can in no way be employed to suggest that widespread settlement within

27 Quoted in Westropp, 'The ancient forts of Ireland', p. 625.   28 Kelly, *Early Irish law*, pp.
257–9; P. Harbison, *Guide to national and historic monuments of Ireland; including a selection of
other monuments not in state care* (Dublin, 1992), see p. 57.   29 H. Long, 'Three settlements
of Gaelic Wicklow' in W. Nolan and K. Hanigan (ed.), *Wicklow: history and society* (Dublin,
1994), pp 237–65, see pp 245–6.

ringforts, and the society which they represent, persisted into post-medieval times. A poem which laments the lost glories of the O'Byrne clan mentions a ringfort along with other pre-Norman possessions which the families had lost over four centuries earlier.[31] This and other late references seem to represent a continuity of the bardic tradition and subject matter rather than, as has been suggested,[32] occupation within ringforts in the sixteenth century.

The function of ringforts as well-defended, dispersed farmsteads is established in contemporary sources and once again confirms many archaeologically derived conclusions. Liability was incurred if destrained livestock were lost owing to the '*dun* not being strong', a reference which indicates that ringforts served as pounds for seized livestock and as such required stout defences.[33] In contrast, there is a dearth of evidence for any unenclosed nucleated population which challenges the *einzelhöfe* model for secular settlement, nor a suggestion that anything other than ringforts constituted the dominant settlement form. There *are* references to land held jointly by the derbhfine,[34] but as co operative land dealings are more litigious than independent farming enterprises, early Irish law might overemphasise the extent and importance of kinlands within the *túath*. There are also references to co-operative farming in *Críth Gablach*; the ócaire and bóaire, the two lowest grades of freemen, are said to have shared ploughing equipment.[35] This may reflect the minor significance of tillage in the secular economy, but it cannot be assumed that co-operative farming indicates any degree of nucleated settlement. Nowhere in the laws is there a description of such a settlement and it is not even 'approximately true' that nucleation was the expression of servile status.[36] The lower grades of society were legally bound to their lord, to the extent that compensation for injury was paid to the lord and not to the family of the injured.[37] All things considered, the location of the lower classes was most likely in close proximity to their lords and not in nucleated settlements isolated from ringforts. The clustering of residences, implied by laws relating to co-operative farming and kin-land, does not imply that houses lay in compact villages, but only that residences were near enough to each other for people to interact regularly.[38]

The location and significance of the *cumal*, or female slaves, is a problematic issue. They were at one time a unit of exchange in Ireland,[39] and it is highly likely

30 G. Hayes-McCoy, *Ulster and other Irish maps* c.*1600* (Dublin, 1964).   **31** Smyth, *Celtic Leinster*, p. 49.   **32** H. Long, 'Three settlements', p. 245.   **33** D. Binchy, 'Distraint in Irish law' in *Celtica*, x (1973), pp 22–71, see p. 46.   **34** Descendants on the male line of the same grandfather; see Kelly, *Early Irish law*, pp 12   **35** MacNeill, 'Ancient Irish law', pp 287, 290.   **36** T. Charles-Edwards, 'The Church and settlement' in P. Ní Chatháin and M. Richter (eds), *Ireland and Europe: the early church* (Stuttgart, 1984), pp 160–75, see pp 170–1.   **37** L. Breatnach, pers. comm.   **38** N. Patterson, *Cattle lords and clansmen: the social structure of early Ireland* (Notre Dame, 1991, 2nd ed.), see p. 109.   **39** Binchy (ed.), *Críth Gablach*, p. 81.

0   50mm

Plate 16   The Lagore hostage collar is a reminder of the sometimes-harsh realities of life
in Early Christian Ireland (National Museum of Ireland).

that they too were located in close proximity to the lords whose status they in part
determined. It is also possible that the cumal, the actual female slave (not her
equivalent value), continued to be a unit of exchange. Society would require a large
number of milkers to drive an economy where the production of dairy products was
of paramount importance. That these were female is con firmed in the lives of the
saints; in one life of Brigit, a man grieves because there is no woman available to do
the milking and a common motif in the lives of the saints has a saint fleeing from
the sound of cows because this also meant the presence of women.[40] The hostage
collar from Lagore crannóg, Meath,[41] is a chilling reminder of the harsher realities
of Early Christian life (plate 16).

What was enclosed within ringforts is similarly well documented in early Irish
law. The dimensions of houses are detailed in the same manner as ringforts, and
they also agree with excavation results. In *Críth Gablach* the different grades are
said to have houses ranging in size from 5.18m (in diameter, although this is not

---

40 R. Sharpe, *Medieval Irish saints' lives: an introduction to* Vitae Sanctorum Hiberniae
(Oxford, 1991), see p. 152; C. Plummer (ed.), *Vitae Sanctorum Hiberniae* (2 vols., Oxford,
1910), see vol. i, p. cxxi.   **41** Mytum, *Origins*, fig. 4:23, p. 144; Scott has suggested that they
may have been intended for hunting dogs.

stated) for an *ócaire* to 11.28m for a king.[42] The most commonly occurring diameter for known Early Christian houses (*c.*6m) is, as would be expected, nearer to the size attributed to typical farmers than high status individuals. The *bóaire feasa* is associated with seven ridge-poles (i.e. individual buildings), a house of 8.23m, an outhouse of 4.57m (presumably attached in the figure-of-eight manner of houses found at Deer Park Farms), a kiln, a barn, a sheep-fold, a calffold and a pigsty.[43] The homes of high status individuals, the *airig*, contained eight beds including a bed for his foster-son, foster-brother, man, wife, son and daughter.[44][44] Perhaps a slave and a grandparent occupied the other two beds. Thus accommodation in the largest houses probably did not exceed eight per sons. In addition to housing and the keeping of livestock, the laws testify to a wide range of everyday human activity that would have taken place within or near a ringfort; tending the sick, cooking, beer making, washing, bathing, visiting, keeping pets, drinking, playing games and musical entertainment.[45]

Early Irish law tracts offer ample confirmation of the mixed economy practised by the contemporary population as well as the primary importance of cattle to the economy and to society as a whole. Cows were the basic determinant of status in this rural society and indeed 'almost had a status as members of society' themselves.[46] Lord/client relationships were cemented through the exchange of cattle.[47] This 'fief – usually of cattle but, as we have seen, sometimes of land as well – was given to a client who, at the end of a year, would pay his lord an annual food-rent based on the size of the original advance. Thus the more cows a person had, the more clients he could maintain and the number of clients and cattle were used as measures of lordly status.[48] Clients were obliged to support their lord in civil and military actions and could, through careful husbandry, use this relationship to advance up the social hierarchy. Although there were severe economic penalties for defaulting on the agreement, either side could terminate the lord/client relationship at any time.[49]

McCormick's confirmation that the composition of the dairy herd from Early Christian excavations mirrored the dairy herd as described in *Críth Gablach*, again testifies to the overall accuracy of Early Irish law.[50] This same law tract states that the *ócaire* would have had an equal number of cows, pigs and sheep.[51] However, as this was the lowest grade of landless freeman, it might not be expected to have a typical holding in livestock. No such claim of equal livestock numbers is made

42 MacNeill, 'Ancient Irish law', pp 287, 305.   43 Ibid., p. 290.   44 Ibid., p. 297.   45 Ibid., pp 285, 287, 291, 299, 304, 306.   46 Lucas, *Cattle in ancient Ireland*, p. 3.   47 N. McLeod, 'Interpreting early Irish law (part 2)', pp 62–3.   48 F. McCormick, 'Exchange of livestock in Early Christian Ireland, AD 450–1150' in *Anthropozoologica*, xvi (1992), pp 31–6. There is no evidence to suggest that higher status ringforts had economies significantly different from more typical sites, but the exchange of cattle and other livestock makes it impossible to be certain to what extent archaeological evidence uncovered from a ringfort reflects the agricultural practices of that particular site, see p. 35.   49 Kelly, *Early Irish law*, pp 29–33.   50 McCormick, 'Dairying and beef production in Early Christian Ireland', pp 256, 259.   51 MacNeill, 'Ancient Irish law', p. 286.

for the independent and more typical *bóaire* grade or any of the higher grades, although they do have a calf-fold, sheep-fold and pigsty, all presumably within their ringforts.

Evidence for tillage is contained within the same legal sources. *Críth Gablach* states that the *ócaire* had a fourth share and the *bóaire* had a half share in a plough, while both had a share in a corn-drying kiln and in a mill.[52] Grindstones and billhooks are also mentioned and these too have been found in ringfort excavations.[53] Higher grades would have had control over milling operations according to this tract and, as some horizontal water milling was in ecclesiastical control, this would have been of significant economic importance to religious communities.[54] The occupants of ringforts also called upon a wide range of foodstuffs to provide a degree of variety in a diet dominated by milk products. Red deer, fish and shellfish remains are commonly found at ringfort excavations.[55] According to early Irish law, hens, geese and bees were also kept. Seven varieties of grain were grown, as well as peas, beans, onions and possibly celery.[56]

A wide range of manufacturing and craft is discussed in Early Irish law, but where the small-scale industrial activity took place is not made clear. The carpenter and blacksmith were hugely significant in rural society, mirrored in the fact that a 'chief expert wright' had an honour price in excess of the highest grade of *brithem* (judge).[57] These high-status craftsmen must have operated from their own ringforts. Excavations which have uncovered large amounts of iron slag could denote the enclosure of a blacksmith, but no site has been identified as the residence of a master carpenter. At the other end of the scale (and a reminder of the small saw from Deer Park Farms) was the comb-maker who was the butt of Early Irish humour:

> Three things confer status on the comb-maker: racing a dog in con
> tending for a bone, straightening the horn of a ram by his breath without
> fire, chanting on a dunghill so that he summons on top what there is
> below of antlers and bones and horns.[58]

The description suggests both a scavenger and a journeyman.

It is not surprising that this agrarian society displayed an acute awareness of environmental factors. Many researchers have shown that farmers often selected the best soils locally available for the location of their ringforts. An explicit statement concerning the value of land is found in the eighth-century law tract *Cis lir fodlaw tire?* (how many kinds of land are there?). Six different types of land are ranked and valued from level arable land at eight *cumal* (or twenty-four cows) to bog at 1.3 *cumal* (or eight dry cows) (table 5).[59] It seems unusual that level land, where

---

52 Ibid., p. 291.   53 Lynn and McDowell, 'Deer Park Farms', p. 24.   54 Mytum, *Origins*, pp 198–9.   55 Proudfoot, 'Economy of the Irish rath', pp 113–5.   56 Fergus Kelly in a lecture on 'Early Irish Farming: the evidence of seventh-eighth century law-texts' (Dublin, 1988).   57 Kelly, Early Irish, law, pp 61–2.   58 Ibid., p. 63.

ringforts are rarely located, is given a higher value than the upland. Perhaps the term 'cultivable' described only the lightest soils, given contemporary ploughing technology. The other values are placed in logical order. Bog land had the lowest value indicating its unsuitability for agriculture and the unimportance of peat as a fuel source in a still heavily wooded countryside. Nonetheless, evidence from Ardee Bog shows that the inhabitants of nearby ringforts harvested peat around AD900.[60]

Table 5
Land values from early Irish law (in cumal)[61]

Description	Value	Description	Value
Level cultivable land	8.0	Rough uncultivable ferny plains	2.7
Upland cultivable land	6.7	Mountain land	2.0
Cultivable land requiring labour	5.3	Bog	1.3

Location factors which, contribute to land value (added values in cumal*)*

Factor	Increase	Factor	Increase
Highway to a lord's dwelling or monastery	1.0	Copper or iron mine	0.8
Sea (with access to 'productive rock')	1.0	Mill	0.8
River	1.0	River mouth	0.8
Mountain	1.0	Pond for cattle	0.4
Enclosed wood (perhaps also enclosed land)	1.7	Road to forest, sea or mountain	0.3
Unenclosed wood	0.8	By-road to cattle pond or remote land	0.2

This legal text also describes various locational attributes, both natural and man-made which contribute to the value of land. These too show an aware ness of environmental factors. Proximity to the sea made possible the collection of seaweed from its 'productive rock' as fertiliser for tillage crops and vegetable gardens, in addition to food resources, especially shellfish, to supplement a diet in which milk products dominated. Dilesk (edible seaweed) is mentioned in *Críth Gablach* and other passages in early Irish law refer to the use of sea sand and shells as an alternative to manuring fields.[62] A river offered a similar contribution to food resources and access to arteries of communication, for as one researcher noted, roads in the Early Christian period were nearly as bad as roads today.[63] Proximity to mountain land permitted extensive summer grazing, or boolying as it is known, a practise well documented in Early Irish sources. This source also recognises the advantages of a cattle-pond which has not gone dry in three generations, as it does land on minor road ways which affords access to these valuable environmental resources.

The high value accorded to land in proximity to woodland displays a recognition

59 G. Mac Niocaill, 'Tír Cumaile' in *Ériu*, xxii (1971), pp 81–6.   **60** F. Mitchell and B. Tuite, *The great bog of Ardee* (Dundalk, 1993), see p. 29, fig. 17.   **61** Based on Mac Niocaill, 'Tír Cumaile', pp 81–6; land values based on McLeod, 'Interpreting early Irish law (part 2)', p. 101.   **62** Ó Cróinín, *Early Medieval Ireland*, pp 92, 104.   **63** T. Barry, pers. comm.

of the valuable resource in terms of both timber for construction and as a fuel source, and in oak woods, mast for grazing pigs. That grazing was of tantamount importance is indicated by a wood's value being determined by the presence or absence of a 'ditch or stone fence ... of legal standard'. However, a later text which addresses the same subject suggests that it was the presence of an enclosure, not the wood, which influenced land values. The lives of the saints describe a landscape which was extensively wooded, especially in Connaught,[64] and the clearance of woodland which was necessary prior to the construction of at least one ecclesiastical enclosure.[65] That some of the Early Christian landscape was enclosed is demonstrated by references in contemporary law to four varieties of fence.[66] But at the same time, much of the land remained unenclosed, especially the upland, giving rise to the common motif in the lives of the saints where the young saint-to-be was employed to keep the calves away from the cows. Finally, the importance of all types of land is summed up in a comment by Saint Maedoc of Ferns, 'Every man of an estate or land is a shanachie';[67] meaning that it was self-interest which made an awareness of the past, especially of family history, essential.

Although there is no explanation for the variation in ringfort density on a national level, certain references help to explain some commonly observed characteristics in that distribution. In many study areas, ringfort builders displayed a preference for well drained slopes as opposed to hilltops or valley bottoms. This location is recognised in a story from the *Book of Lismore*:

> Still they advance, and so to a wide smooth plain clad in flowering clover
> all bedewed with honey; a perfectly flat and even plain it was, without
> either rise or fall of surfaces except three prominent hills that it bore,
> each one of these having on its side an impregnable dún.[68]

The strategic advantages of a hill-slope location, as opposed to a hill top one where ringforts are seldom found, is provided in the rather warlike life of Saint Findchua. Preparing for battle against the Ulstermen, Findchua built a palisade defence downslope from his opponents and let them charge from the top of the hill.[69] Advantage was gained, presumably, by the inability of the Ulstermen to control their advance corning down slope, while an upslope attack would have been equally problematic.

Accepting that predominantly pastoral based communities chose the best

64 Plummer (ed.), *Vitae Sanctorum Hiberniae*, vol. i, p. civ.   65 Plummer (ed. and trans.), *Bethada Náem nÉrenn*. p. 292.   66 D. Ó Corráin, 'Some legal references to fences and fencing in Early Historic Ireland' in Reeves-Smyth and Hamond (eds), *Landscape archaeology*, pp 247–52.   67 Plummer (ed. and trans.), *Bethada Náem nÉrenn*, p. 240.   68 S. O'Grady (ed. and trans.), 'The adventure of Cian's son Teigue' in *Silva Gadelica, (i–xxxi): a collection of tales in Irish with extracts illustrating persons and places* (London, 1892).   69 W. Stokes (ed. and trans.), *Lives of the saints from the Book of Lismore* (Oxford, 1890), see p. 240.

farming locations, settlement models seek to explain distribution patterns within environmentally favoured areas, with special reference to the inter-relationship between ringforts and their occupants. One such model, although based entirely on contemporary sources, predicted models derived from field evidence which show the spatial relationships of ringforts belonging to different grades (fig. 31).[70] Simms proposed that the lord/client relationship would dictate the location of persons within a túath and (in my view) the location of their ringforts.

In the law tracts there are some indications of the siting of enclosed farm steads within holdings. Legal references established the need to locate a pound for distrained livestock away from borders, and further associates the highest status lord with this function: 'the distress of a kinsman-surety is brought into the green of an *aire forgill*.[71] Allusion to the military functions of the *aire forgill* and *aire* ard also convey information about their central location within a túath; 'the *ánsruth* (a term which McLeod equates with these high status lords), i.e. a man who protects his district and its border; the wounding of a person [is common] for him in each of the four seasons of the year ... he protects its border to its four compass points with battle ...'[72] The defence of both district and all borders would necessitate a central location. In the south-west midlands, 'high status' bivallate enclosures with smaller than average interiors were the most centrally located (within townlands) of all five ringfort divisions (figs 26, 33).[73] In contrast the lord with lowest status, the *aire déso* (which McLeod equates with the *aire échta*, the lord of vengeance)[74] seems to have functioned as a military leader in inter-territorial conflicts. 'He is a leader ... who is left to do feats of arms in [a neighbouring territory under] treaty-law ... to avenge an offence against the honour of the *túath*'.[75] This description would suggest a peripheral location for the ringforts of an *aire déso*. In the south-west midlands large, well defended 'multi-functional' ringforts were most peripherally located (within townlands) and were consistently located in strategic boundary locations.[76] The association between this ringfort class and boundaries was also noted elsewhere in Offaly. At the other end of the social scale, it has been seen how *ócaire* clients were associated with smaller ringforts consistent with the limited investment probable on rented property. Their ringforts were located on 13.9ha land units probably rented from lordly grades with surplus land. In spatial terms, this would locate the farmsteads of the *ócaire* in close proximity to the more prominent members of Early Christian society in contrast to the economically and spatially independent *bóaire*. The association between 'high-status' ringforts and the least substantial Cluster 5 examples was noted throughout the south-west midlands. They are the

70 A. Simms, 'Continuity and change: settlement and society in medieval Ireland *c.*500–1500' in W. Nolan (ed.), *The shaping of Ireland: the geographical perspective* (Cork, 1986), pp 44–65.   71 Binchy, 'Distraint in Irish law', p. 46.   72 McLeod, 'Interpreting early Irish law (part 2)', pp 44–5.   73 M. Stout, 'Ringforts', pp 231–2.   74 McLeod, 'Interpreting early Irish law (part 2)', pp 50–1.   75 MacNeill, 'Ancient Irish law', p. 297.   76 M. Stout, 'Ringforts', p. 232.

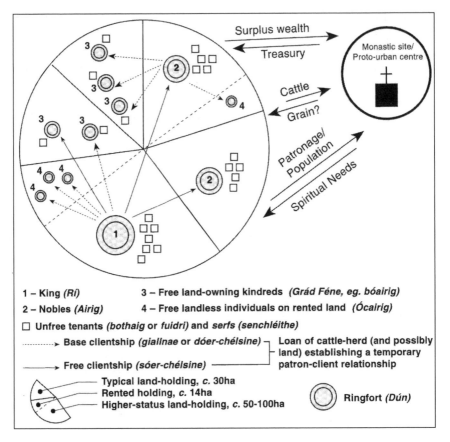

Figure 31   Model of an Early Christian túath based on contemporary law tracts. This
model highlights the inter-relationships of ringfort dwelling freemen and
the mutually advantageous links between ecclesiastical and secular settlement
(After Simms, 1986; with additions by the author).

most likely ringfort class to have enclosed the semi-permanent, insecure farming
enterprises of the *ócaire* as outlined in the law tracts.

That a relationship between ringforts did exist is implicit in the popular
belief that each ringfort has a view of five neighbouring enclosures. The inter-
relationships of a hierarchy or ringforts was articulated as early as 1821 when a
model of ringfort distribution was published for 'the south of Ireland' (fig. 32):

> The principal fort is placed in the centre of subordinate ones … a fort
> was thus encompassed; each of the small ones is situate within a quarter
> of a mile. The central position of the rath rendered it secure, while its
> situation on a commanding height enabled the chieftain, not only to see
> the point of attack, but to muster his forces speedily; while on the other

In some parts of the south of Ireland, the rath or principal fort is placed in the centre of subordinate ones, each of which is called *lios*, as in the following sketch :

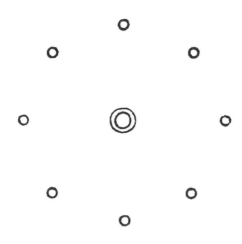

In the neighbourhood of my residence, a fort called *rath Piola'id*, which means the chieftain's or prince's fortification, was thus encompassed : each of the small ones is

Figure 32 This 1821 description of Early Christian secular settlement is a precursor of recent hierarchical and defensive models. Wood wrote; 'the principal fort is placed in the centre of subordinate ones ... The central position of the rath rendered it secure, while its situation on a commanding height enabled the chieftain, not only to see the point of attack, but to muster his forces speedily ... (Wood, 1821, p. 269).

hand, every surrounding fort in danger, being equidistant from the rath, possessed every advantage from a situation which could be expected from the vicinity, skill and orders of the chieftain.[77]

This describes a similar situation as that identified by Warner in Clogher, Tyrone (as shown above) where a royal ringfort was surrounded by ringforts of lower status. In the south-west midlands, just as it was possible to construct a normative model which summarised the distribution of ringforts today (fig. 26), so too has a hypothetical model been constructed which suggests from what basis this distribution developed (fig. 33): On well-drained slopes above 152m, an *aire forgill* has a holding of approximately six *tír cumaile* (83.4ha). The area is strategically sited, having a commanding view of the countryside below it and a location near an artery of communication. Most of the land belonging to this lord is 'rented' to *ócaire*, the sons of nobility or other landless freeman. The farmstead of an *aire déso* is sited in more level terrain near the *túath* boundary in accordance with the inter-territorial functions of this class. Three quarters of the cleared and enclosed land associated with this lord is farmed directly by him. This is in contrast to the *aire forgill* and demonstrates the lower status of the *aire déso*. The independent farmsteads of the *bóaire* are strung out along well-drained slopes above the 122m contour. Although these men owe allegiance to one or both of these neighbouring lords, they farm the land which they and their immediate families possess outright. It is possible that the boundaries of these farms roughly correspond with modern townland boundaries and that it was from these typical farming units that the modern townland framework developed. Large uninhabited regions in this model indicate that some land was either farmed in common or remained an area of extensive woodland.

To a certain extent, the same model could be applied to north Roscommon by reversing the contours. The juxtaposition of ringforts associated with high and low status individuals also occurs, albeit in a low-lying location. A key difference lies in the fact that a much smaller percentage of high-status individuals (6%) and a larger percentage of individuals of low-status (40%) are indicated by the ringfort classifications. North Roscommon was more densely populated than the south-west midlands, and critically, was a long-established royal residence and inauguration site for the kings of Connaught. Perhaps the distribution of ringforts reflects a more polarised society: the haves were fewer but richer, perhaps even provincial kings; the have-nots were more numerous and poorer, *ócaire* and lower status *bóaire* dwelling in ringforts smaller even than the farmsteads of their equivalent grade in the south-west midlands. Most of the more typical farming enterprises, associated with *bóaire* and lower level aire, took place on sloping farmland at some remove

---

77 T. Wood, *An inquiry concerning the primitive inhabitants of Ireland* (Cork, 1821), seep. 269. My thanks to Rolf Loeber for bringing this early reference to my attention.

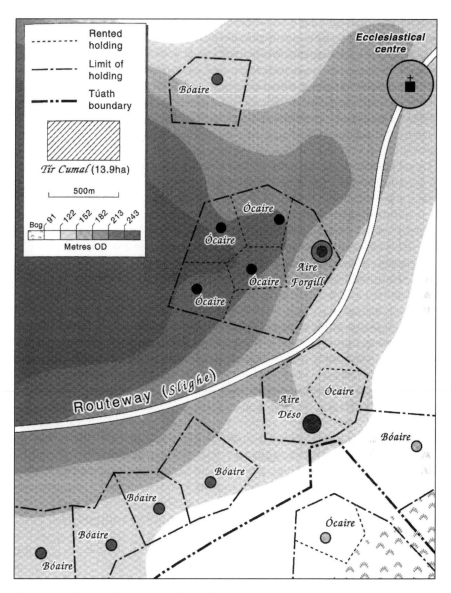

Figure 33 Hypothetical model of Early Christian settlement based on the law tracts and the existing distribution of ringforts, ecclesiastical sites, territorial boundaries and topography in the south-west midlands. The size of the tír cumal, the basic unit of land measurement, is indicated in the key.

from high status locations.

The dichotomy between the distribution of ecclesiastical sites and ringforts apparent in the landscape is well evidenced in the lives of the saints. They are also particularly revealing about the tensions which arose between the early church and secular powers. In a life of Patrick it is clear that, although the ecclesiastic wanted an upland location for his ecclesiastical site, the secular powers originally insisted on a low-lying, less favourable site:

> Thereafter Patrick, at the angel's word, went to the Macha, to the place wherein Raith Dáire stands today. There was a certain wealthy and venerable man, name Dáire at that time in Orior. Patrick asked this Dáire to give him a site for his church on Druim Sailech, the stead whereon Armagh stands today. Dáire said that he would not give him the hill, but that he would give him a site in the valley were the Ferta stands today ... Dáire and his wife afterwards went wholly in accordance with Patrick's will and they offered him ... the hill for which had previously asked, which is named Armagh today.[78]

A brave face was put on this locationally inferior status. In a life of Ciarán of Clonmacnoise, the saint says 'if it were here [at Clonmacnoise] that I were, though this stead were low as regards to place, it would be high as regards honour and reverence'.[79] Something of a similar vein is seen in an extract from the life of Berach. Patrick is said to have prophesied the location of that future saint's monastery:

> Then Patrick ordained that it should be in the meadow on the brink of the lake that the son of promise [Berach] should build his city and he ordered that its sanctuary ground should be all that lies between the bog and the lake, that is the plain with its woody meadows and boggy oak groves. Then said the chieftain to Patrick "Difficult is the place of abode". Patrick said "that which is difficult with men, is easy with god".[80]

Mochuda described the low-lying landscape of Rahan in the following terms: 'Glorious Rahan, evident its riches. Above the cleared forest of the tribe of Ere; This is what I compare Rahan to, to a meadow of the plain of heaven'.[81] Although this low-lying location forced the church to accept certain environ mental disadvantages, Bitel has pointed out that church foundations, far from being isolated communities, chose [or were obliged to accept] riverine locations and sites near harbours to facilitate labourers and traders.[82] Unlike most ringforts, which had no central place functions, the contemporary sources show how ecclesiastical

---

78 78 Stokes (ed. and trans.), *Saints from the Book of Lismore*, p. 165.   79 Ibid., p. 274.   80 Plummer (ed. and trans.), *Bethada Náem nÉrenn*, vol. i., p. 24.   81 Ibid., p. 304.   82 L. Bitel, *Isle of the saints; monastic settlement and Christian community in early Ireland*, second ed. (Cork, 1994).

sites developed into proto-urban centres, becoming the site of fairs in response to the need for local exchange from the eighth century.[83] That they were centres of learning and craftsmanship is well attested. They may also have functioned as secure places for secular wealth. At Rahan, some cows were 'carried off ... from the middle of the cemetery'. After this the man who owned the cows, rather than the church itself, killed the thief.[84]

The worldly ways of the early church in Ireland are well demonstrated in the lives of saints. Saint Attracta vowed not to settle except where seven roads met.[85] Saint Crónán, who move his early isolated church at Sean Ross to a new location in Roscrea on the Slighe Dála (one of the five main roads in Early Christian Ireland),[86] chastised Saint Mochuda for his isolation; 'To a man who avoids guests and builds his church in a wild bog, away from the level road, I will not go; but let him have beasts of the wilderness for his guests'.[87] Analysis of Early Christian settlement in Offaly drew attention the importance of routeways as a determinant of distribution; ecclesiastical sites were located on routeways (the Brosna, Escir Riada and midland corridor) while they were shunned by ringfort builders, especially most of those sites associated with highest status occupants (see above, chapter 6). Roads made a major contribution to land values, especially *slighe* which gave access to a lord's ringfort or to a monastery (see table 5). It is significant that it is accessibility rather than proximity to a monastery that is valuable, comparing well with the Offaly results. Routeways, especially rivers, often formed important boundaries in the Early Christian landscape and as ecclesiastical sites were commonly located on boundaries.[88] Their riverine distribution has a strategic as well as an economic significance.

An economic dichotomy, mirroring locational ones, is also suggested in the saints lives. There is a strong association between the early church and milling, and the chief economic activities are tillage-based. It was noted above (chapter 5) that the foundation of an ecclesiastical site on Inishbofin may have influenced a shift from a pastoral based to a tillage-based economy. An explicit link between the tillage economy and the church is made in a vision which seems to describe cross-ploughing, necessary before the introduction of the mould board plough *c*.AD600:

> "I beheld" saith Brigit, "four ploughs in the south-east, which ploughed the whole island, and before the sowing was finished, the harvest was ripened, and clear well-springs and shining streams came out of the

83 C. Doherty, 'Some aspects of hagiography as a source for Irish economic history' in *Peritia*, i (1982), pp 300–28, see p. 302. 84 Plummer, *Bethada Náem nÉrenn*, p. 306. 85 Plummer (ed.), *Vitae Sanctorum Hiberniae*, vol. i, p. cxiii · 86 From the Latin life of St Cronan, see D. Gleeson, *Roscrea: town and parish* (Dublin, 1947), p. 7; See also G. Stout, *Ikerrin*, pp 96, 101–2. 87 Bitel, *Isle of saints*, p. 38. 88 P. Ó Riain, 'Boundary association in Early Irish society' in *Studia Celtica*, vii (1972), pp 12–29, see pp 17–19.

furrows. White garments were on the sowers and ploughmen. I beheld four other ploughs in the north, which ploughed the island athwart, and turned the harvest again, and the oats which they had sown grew up at once, and was ripe, and black streams came out of the furrows, and there were black garments on the sowers and the ploughmen." "That is not difficult", saith Patrick. "The first four ploughs which thou beheldest, those are I and thou, who sow the four books of the Gospel with a sowing of faith, and belief, and piety. The harvest which thou beheldest are they who come onto that faith and belief through our teaching. The four ploughs which thou beheldest in the north are the false teachers and the liars who will overturn the teaching which we are sowing."[89]

Again, this dichotomy is seen in the early years of many saints who, as children, perform miraculous tasks while engaged in pastoral activity but performed miracles associated with tillage after joining the church. For example, the first miracle Colum Cille performed after he founded Raphoe was to bring back to life the mill wright who had drowned in the millpond. Before joining the church Brigit tended sheep, cows and pigs and there is an account of visiting her mother, a bondswoman (*ndoeire*) in a mountain dairy or *buaile*. But after joining the church Brigit's first agricultural reference is to her brewing beer and it is said that 'there did not happen to be a cow in the church at that time'.[90] These tales place the young saints-to-be in the economic mainstream, establishing their credentials as representative members of a dominantly pastoral society before finding a new life in the church where tillage seems to dominate.

89 Stokes, *Saints from the Book of Lismore*, pp 192–3. J. Andrews, pers. comm., has pointed out that in this passage cross-ploughing was abnormal and deplorable. Perhaps the tale dates from a period soon after the introduction of the mouldboard plough.   90 Stokes (ed. and trans.), *Saints from the Book of Lismore*, pp 186–9.

Conclusions

Saint Patrick, who was himself 'imported' as a slave from Britain in his youth, is said to have returned to Ireland in 432 to spread the Christian faith; an event redolent of a complex chain of events, of innovation and exchange which gave rise to the Early Christian period as we know it. The introduction of Christianity was but one aspect of a *kulturebundle* that resulted from contacts with the Roman world; an exchange of materials and ideas crossing to and fro across the Irish Sea, which must not be seen a barrier, but rather as a unifying artery of communication during this period. Innovations included literacy, which meant that during the first millennium, Ireland gradually emerges from pre-history into history; improved technology and farming methods, which resulted in a better diet and, presumably, a healthier, longer-lived people; and monastic organisation, which permitted the concentration of a large work force and the exploitation of land and labour resources in an unique way. The improvements resulted in an huge upsurge in population which had profound landscape consequences, most particularly the construction of over 47,000 enclosed farmsteads.

These ringforts were most likely built over a relatively short period of perhaps three centuries. This fact, and the possibility that today's distribution of enclosures may reflect their original location and relative density, support one of the most important assumptions in the above analysis, that ringforts were roughly contemporary with one-another. While the outline provided of their distribution pattern remains valid, all the conclusions based on the distribution of ringforts stand or fall on the validity of this one assumption. Accepting contemporaneity permits a meaningful interpretation of the relationship of different types of ringforts in the Irish landscape. The hierarchy of sites, which intuitively suggests that individuals with a wide range of status were housed within ringforts, is confirmed in the laws which describe larger, bivallate sites as the homes of kings, leaving smaller less impressive ringforts to be associated with the lesser ranks of society, also detailed in Early Irish law. The relationship between different elements in that society pre-supposed a certain spatial arrangement, and this was confirmed in detailed studies of ringforts in the south-west midlands and in north Roscommon. The complementary distribution of ringforts and ecclesiastical sites is another conclusion drawn from a large number of settlement studies. Here again, contemporary and near contemporary accounts support these findings. The lives of the saints point to tension which arose in society with the introduction of

Christianity. The church had to be provided with land and these sources suggest that it was the secular power which determined the location of that land, locations which even then were often recognised as being deficient.

Analysis of distribution is but one aspect of Early Christian studies which combine to reinforce the findings of various disciplines. Archaeology and archaeozoology are critical to our knowledge about the chronology of ringforts and how their occupants lived. The analysis of bones from excavated Early Christian sites show the dominance of cattle in the diet and the concentration of dairying which is mirrored in the law tracts. Even the size of houses within ringforts, known from excavations, correspond with the measures given in *Críth Gablach* and, like ringfort diameters, point to a wide range in the status of individuals which inhabited these farmsteads.

We have seen that from a lull in the later Iron Age there was an upsurge in agricultural activity resulting in widespread forest clearance. Mitchell has convincingly linked this activity to the introduction of the coulter plough around AD300, and the mouldboard plough around AD600. In addition, the horizontal mill also makes an appearance around AD600. Cumulatively, these advances represent a technological revolution permitting grain production on an industrial scale. It had always been a puzzle how, if these technological strides forward took place in the tillage fields, livestock rearing retained a primary position in the secular economy and culture. In my view, this was partly made possible by the link between intensive tillage and the church. If monasteries were the main grain producers, it would explain their low-lying position (to avail of water power); a position made tenable by improved ploughing technology which could exploit heavier lowland soils. The church could, therefore, dovetail nicely into a pre-existing society located primarily on the better drained upland where cattle remained king. This symbiotic relationship between secular and ecclesiastical economies goes a long way towards explaining why there were no martyrs in Early Irish church history.

These tentative conclusions become more convincing in the light of McCormick's ground-breaking analysis which added dairying to the techno logical advances which were introduced or developed in Ireland at this time. A society which had already put the acquisition of cattle to the fore in the pre historic Iron Age found that with the development of dairying the food value of their livestock improved four-fold.[1] Improved diet inevitably led to an upsurge in population in both people and cattle, ultimately giving rise to the need for the thousands of ringforts which came to be constructed. More settlement meant more clearance, and ever-increasing production. It is this upsurge in population and surplus wealth which provided the patronage for monasteries, enabling their development into centres of learning and craftsmanship. Thus, to find the origins of the great

---

1 McCormick, 'Cows, ringforts and the origins of Early Christian Ireland', p. 35.

flowering of Irish civilisation we must look, usually upslope, from the fabulous church remains to the anonymous ringforts wherein dwelt the individuals with real power in Early Christian society.

The wealth of information which can be obtained from surviving settlement evidence shows the importance of preserving our Early Christian heritage. Vast sums are spent, and correctly so, on preserving the ecclesiastical component of that heritage. But this takes place against a background of the continued largescale destruction of the all important, but less spectacular, secular settlements. Ringforts have been destroyed in their thousands since being comprehensively mapped in the 1840s. Much of this destructive orgy took place in recent times when the EU financed a short-sighted programme of farm development. Large grants and large machines created the large fields which annihilated the rich grassland archaeology in much of Ireland. A c.37% destruction rate of all earth works mapped on the various OS editions is a preliminary estimate based on the many archaeological surveys now available.[2] More recently, ringforts located in marginal areas, especially uplands immediately below the 300m contour, have been threatened by afforestation. It is hoped that the recent European trend towards extensification rather than intensification in farming will lessen the threat to these vulnerable sites. The Rural Environmental Protection Scheme (REPS) should be deployed to ensure the preservation of ringforts in the Irish countryside by encouraging farmers, through grant-aid, to preserve archaeological monuments on their land. Another welcome development in recent legislation in the Republic gives legal status to all archaeological features listed in the Sites and Monuments Records, including all upstanding ringforts and the known sites of destroyed enclosures.

Along with greater protection, recent trends point to a greater appreciation of what exactly ringforts represent. It is difficult to imagine how a ringfort originally looked or functioned by simply examining the upstanding remains; this may in part explain why so little controversy accompanied their mass destruction. Attempts at ringfort reconstructions have made it possible for the wider public to visualise these monuments. Two projects have involved the excavation of a ringfort prior to the reconstruction of the exposed features in situ, including souterrains and houses.[3] Other reconstructions have been based on an amalgam of excavation

---

2 This crude measure is derived be comparing the number of positively identified ringforts with enclosures (in most cases destroyed ringforts) in those counties where preliminary field inspections have been completed. Longford had a destruction rate of 3%, Westmeath 3%, Cavan 4%, Monaghan 12%, Fermanagh 18%, Galway 27%, Meath 29%, Donegal 39%, Cork 39%, Louth 45%, Tyrone 52%, Carlow 61%, Antrim 66%, Kildare 66%, Down 79%, Derry 80%. More detailed analysis of destruction rates yielded the following results: 11% in sampled areas of Leitrim, see Farrelly, Sample study, p. 23. 38% in Ikerrin, Tipperary, see G. Stout, *Ikerrin*, p. 5; 41% in north Kerry, see Toal, *North Kerry*, p. 82; 44% in Dingle, Kerry, see Barrett, The ringfort.   3 J. O'Sullivan, 'The Lisnagun project' in *Archaeology Ireland*, iv (1990), pp 23–5; Erin Gibbons, pers. comm., on the excavation and reconstruction of the cashel at Ballynavenooragh townland on the Dingle peninsula in Kerry.

results, but favouring the handful of ringforts with evidence for elaborate defences and gateways. The end result is often more reminiscent of forts in the American west than Early Christian farms. Nonetheless, the size of the interiors and the number of buildings enclosed does give the modern traveller to the Early Christian past an inkling of how efficient and secure the Irish ringforts were. At Craggaunowen this appreciation is further enhanced with the re-enactment of common domestic activities like spinning, weaving and grinding of corn within their reconstructed enclosures.

If this study has anything in common with Westropp's seminal 1902 study, it is its preliminary nature and the hope that it might direct the course of future research, especially in terms of the analysis of ringfort distribution. Certain areas emerge from this study which demand further attention. The area of very high density in Sligo needs to be examined, as does the relationship between the cashels in the Burren and ringforts further south in west Clare. Another potentially profitable field of research would be to re-examine the geographical context of published (and the many unpublished) ringfort excavations to assess their relationship to adjacent ringforts and ecclesiastical settlement. Proper sampling procedures need to be applied to these geographical studies so that in future, when we are told that 90% of sites are within 300m of a townland boundary, or that 50% of ringforts are above the 200m contour, etc., we are also informed how these figures differ from the results garnered from a random sample of points. Studies of just a few OS 1:10,560 sheets are often more enlightening than more superficial county-wide studies. The analysis of the distribution of ringforts in Ireland presents challenging opportunities to both geographers and landscape archaeologists, requiring an interdisciplinary approach to tease out statistical, archaeological, environmental, linguistic and historic issues – the type of study fostered by the Group for the Study of Irish Historical Settlement.

Bibliography

Aalen, F. and Whelan, K. (ed.) 1992 *Dublin from prehistory to present: studies in honour of J.H. Andrews*, Dublin.

Ancient laws of Ireland, 1865–1901 Hancock, W. *et al.* (ed. and trans.), 5 vols., Dublin.

Association of Young Irish Archaeologists 1972 *Excavations 1971*, Belfast.

Atkinson, J., Banks, I. and O'Sullivan, J. (ed.) 1996 *Nationalism and archaeology*, Glasgow.

Avery, M. 1991–2 'Caiseal na nDuini and Cashelreagan: two forts in Rosguill, county Donegal' in *Ulster Journal of Archaeology*, liv–lv, pp 120–8.

Baillie, M. 1979 'An interim statement on dendrochronology at Belfast', in *Ulster Journal of Archaeology*, xiii, pp 72–84.

— 1992 'Dating the past' in M. Ryan (ed.) *The illustrated archaeology of Ireland*, Dublin, pp 15–19.

Barrett, G. 1972 'The ring-fort: a study in settlement geography with special reference to southern county Donegal and the Dingle area, county Kerry', unpublished Ph.D. thesis. The Queen's University of Belfast.

— 1980 'A field survey and morphological study of ring-forts in southern county Donegal' in Ulster Journal of Archaeology, xliv, pp 39–51

— 1982 'Problems of spatial and temporal continuity of rural settlement in Ireland, A.D. 400 to 1169' in *Journal of Historical Geography*, viii, pp 245–60.

— 1995 'Recovering the hidden archaeology of Ireland: the impact of aerial survey in the River Barrow valley, 1989–91' in *Forschungen zur Archäologie im Land Brandenburg*, iii, pp 45–60.

— and Graham, B. 1975 'Some consideration concerning the dating and distribution of ringforts in Ireland' in *Ulster Journal of Archaeology*, xxxix, pp 33–45.

Barry, T. 1977 *Medieval moated sites of south-east Ireland*, Oxford.

Bennett, I. 1989 'The settlement pattern of ringforts in county Wexford' in *Journal of the Royal Society of Antiquaries of Ireland*, cxix, pp 50–61.

Binchy, D. (ed.) 1941 *Críth Gablach*. Dublin.

— 1973 'Distraint in Irish law' in *Celtica*, x, pp 22–71.

Bitel, L. 1990 *Isle of the saints. Monastic settlement and Christian community in Early Ireland*. 2nd ed. Cork.

Black, L. 1994 'Early Christian settlement in the Braid and Upper Glenarm valleys', unpublished BA thesis, The Queen's University of Belfast.

Bradley, J. 1991 'Excavations at Moynagh Lough, county Meath' in *Journal of the Royal Society of Antiquaries of Ireland*, cxxi., pp 5–26.

— (ed.) 1988 *Settlement and society in Medieval Ireland: studies presented to F. X. Martin*. Kilkenny.

Brady, N. 1983 'An analysis of the spatial distribution of early historic settlement sites in the barony of Morgallion, county Meath', unpublished BA dissertation. University College Dublin.

Brannon, N. 1981–2 'A rescue excavation at Lisdoo Fort, Lisnaskea, county Fermanagh' in *Ulster Journal of Archaeology*, xliv–v, pp 53–9.

Brindley, A. 1986 *Archaeological inventory of county Monaghan*. Dublin.

Buckley, V. and Sweetman, P. 1991 *Archaeological survey of county Louth*. Dublin.

Burenhult, G. 1984 *The archaeology of Carrowmore: environmental archaeology and the megalithic tradition at Carrowmore, county Sligo, Ireland*. Stockholm.

Casselberry, S. 1974 'Further refinement of formulae for determining population from floor area' in *World Archaeology*, vi, 118–22.

Caulfield, S. 1981 'Celtic problems in the Irish Iron Age' in D. Ó Corráin (ed.), *Irish antiquity*. Cork.

Chang, K. 1958 'Study of the Neolithic social grouping: examples from the New World', *American Anthropologist*, lx, 298–334.

Charles-Edwards, T. 1984 'The church and settlement' in P. Ní Chatháin and M. Richter (ed.), *Ireland and Europe: the early church*, Stuttgart, pp 160–75.

— 1986 '*Críth Gablach* and the law of status' in *Peritia*, v, pp 53–73.

Cleary, R., Hurley, M. and Twohig, E. (eds), 1987 *Archaeological excavations on the Cork–Dublin gas pipeline* (1981–82), Cork.

Colfer, B. 1987 'Anglo-Norman settlement in county Wexford', in K. Whelan (ed.), *Wexford: history and society*, Dublin, pp 56–101.

Collins, A. 1966 'Excavations at Dressogagh rath' in *Ulster Journal of Archaeology*, xxix, pp 117–29.

Condit, T. and Gibbons, M. 1990 'A bird's eye view of our past' in *Technology Ireland*, xii, pp 50–4.

Costello, C. 1974 *Ireland and the Holy Land*, Dublin.

Cotter, C. (ed.) 1986 *Excavations 1985*, Dublin.

Coxon, P. and O'Connell, M. (ed.) 1994 *Clare Island and Inishbofin* (Irish Association for Quaternary Studies, field guide no. 17). Dublin.

Crabtree, P. and Ryan, K. (eds) 1991 *Animal use and culture change, MASCA research papers in science and archaeology* (supplement to) viii, Philadelphia, 1991.

Culleton, E. and Mitchell, F. 1976 'Soil erosion following deforestation in the Early Christian period in south Wexford' in *Journal of the Royal Society of Antiquaries of Ireland*, cvi, pp 120–3.

Curtis, E. 1934 'Rental of the manor of Lisronagh, 1333, and notes on 'betagh' tenure in medieval Ireland' in *Proceedings of the Royal Irish Academy*, xliii, C, pp 41–76.

Davies, O. 1937–40 'Excavations at Lissachiggel' in *County Louth Archaeological Journal*, ix, pp 209–43.

— 1940 'Appendix' in E. Watson, 'Prehistoric sites in south Antrim' in *Ulster Journal of Archaeology*, iii (1940), p. 151.

de Paor, M. and de Paor, L. 1961 *Early Christian Ireland*. London

Doherty, C. 1982 'Some aspects of hagiography as a source for Irish economic history' in *Peritia*, i, pp 300–28.

Doody, M. 1993 'Ballyhoura Hills project; Interim report' in *Discovery Programme reports: 1; Project results 1992*, Dublin, pp 20–30.

Driscoll, S. and Nieke, M. (eds) 1988 *Power and politics in early medieval Britain and Ireland*. Edinburgh.

Edwards, N. 1990 *The archaeology of Early Medieval Ireland*. London.

Evans, E. 1952 'Excavations at Mount Royal and Ballysillan, county Antrim' in *Ulster Journal of Archaeology*, xv, pp 84–6;

— and Gaffikin, M. 1935 'Belfast Naturalist's Field Club survey of antiquities: megaliths and raths' in *Irish Naturalist's Journal*, v, pp 242–52.

Fahy, E. 1969 'Early settlement in the Skibbereen area' in *Journal of the Cork archaeological and historical society*, lxxiv, pp 147–56.

Farrelly, J. 1989 'A sample study of ringforts in county Leitrim', unpublished M.A. thesis, University College Dublin.

Finch, T. and Ryan, P. 1966 *Soils of county Limerick*, Dublin.

Gleeson, D. 1947 *Roscrea: town and parish*, Dublin.

Gibbons, M. 1994 'Inishbofin: archaeology and history' in Coxon and O'Connell (eds), *Clare Island and Inishbofin*. Dublin, pp 54–9.

Gowan, M. 1988 *Three Irish gas pipelines: new archaeological evidence in Munster*, Dublin.

— 1992 'Excavations of two souterrain complexes at Marshes Upper, Dundalk, county Louth' in *Proceedings of the Royal Irish Academy*, xcii, C, 55–121.

Harbison, P. 1992 *Guide to national and historic monuments of Ireland; including a selection of other monuments not in state care*, Dublin.

Harper, A. 1974–5 'The excavation of a rath in Crossnacreevy townland, county Down' in *Ulster Journal of Archaeology*, xxxvi–vii, pp 32–41.

Hayes-McCoy, G. 1964 *Ulster and other Irish maps c.1600*, Dublin.

Hennessy, M. 1981 'Territorial organisation in the barony of Burren, county Clare', unpublished BA thesis. University College Dublin.

Herity, M. 1983 'A survey of the royal site of Cruachain in Connaught I: Introduction, the monuments and topography' in *Journal of the Royal Society of Antiquaries of Ireland*, cxiii, pp 121–42.

— 1987 'A survey of the royal site of Cruachain in Connacht III: Ringforts and ecclesiastical sites' in *Journal of the Royal Society of Antiquaries of Ireland*, cxvii, pp 125–41.

— 1988 'A survey of the royal site of Cruachain in Connaught IV: Ancient field systems at Rathcroghan and Carnfree' in *Journal of the Royal Society of Antiquaries of Ireland*, cxviii, pp 67–84.

Hurley, M. 1987 'Garrynatemple, Grange, county Tipperary' in Cleary, Hurley and Twohig (eds), *Cork–Dublin gas pipeline*, Cork, pp 65–70.

Ivens, R. 1984 'Killyliss rath, county Tyrone' in *Ulster Journal of Archaeology*, xlvii, pp 9–35.

Jelicic, L. and O'Connell, M. 1992 'History of vegetation and land use from 3200 B.P. to the present in the north-west Burren, a karstic region of western Ireland' in *Vegetation History and Archaeobotany*, i, pp 119–40.

Jope, E. (ed.) 1966 *An archaeological survey of county Down*. Belfast.

Keegan, M. 1994 'Ringforts in north county Roscommon', unpublished BSc thesis, The Queen's University of Belfast.

Kelly, F. 1988 *A guide to early Irish law*. Dublin.

Kenward, H. and Allison, E. 1994 'A preliminary view of the insect assemblages from the early Christian rath site at Deer Park Farms, Northern Ireland' in J. Rackham (ed.), *Environment and economy in Anglo-Saxon England*, York, pp 89–103.

Lacy, B. *et al.* 1983 *Archaeological survey of county Donegal*. Lifford.

Lamb, H. 1995 *Climate, history and the modern world*. London.

Long, H. 1994 'Three settlements of Gaelic Wicklow' in W. Nolan and K. Hanigan (eds), *Wicklow: history and society*, Dublin, pp 237–65.

Lucas, A. 1989 *Cattle in ancient Ireland*. Kilkenny.

Lynch, A. 1981 *Man and environment in south-west Ireland, 4,000 B.C.–A.D. 800; a study of man's impact on the development of soil and vegetation*, Oxford.

Lynn, C. 1975 'The dating of raths: an orthodox view' in *Ulster Journal of Archaeology*, xxxix, pp 45–7.

— 1978 'A rath in Seacash townland, county Antrim' in *Ulster Journal of Archaeology*, xli, pp 55–74.

— 1980 'The excavation of an earthwork enclosure at Ballynoe, county Antrim', in *Ulster Journal of Archaeology*, xliii, pp 29–38.

— 1981–2 'The excavation of Rathmullan, a raised rath and motte in county Down' in *Ulster Journal of Archaeology*, xliv–v, pp 65–171.

— 1983 'Two raths at Ballyhenry, county Antrim' in *Ulster Journal of Archaeology*, xlvi, pp 67–91.

— 1983 'Some 'early' ring-forts and crann6gs' in *Journal of Irish Archaeology*, i, pp 47– 58.

— 1985 'The excavation of Rathmullan, county Down: Addenda' in *Ulster Journal of Archaeology*, xlviii, pp 130–1.

— 1986 'Deer Park Farms' in C. Cotter (ed.), Excavations 1985, Dublin. pp 9–10.

— 1986 Houses and other related outbuildings in Early Christian Ireland, unpublished PhD thesis, 2 vols. University College Dublin.

— 1987 'Deer Park Farms, Glenarm, county Antrim' in *Archaeology Ireland*, i, pp 11– 15.

— and McDowell, J. 1989 'Deer Park Farms report project' in *IAPA Newsletter*, x, pp 23–4.

McCormick, F. 1983 'Dairying and beef production in Early Christian Ireland, the faunal evidence', in T. Reeves-Smyth and F. Hamond (eds) *Landscape Archaeology in Ireland*, Oxford, pp 253–67.

— 1991 'The effects of the Anglo-Norman settlement on Ireland's wild and domesticated fauna' in P. Crabtree and K. Ryan (eds), *Animal use and culture change, MASCA research papers in science and archaeology* (supplement to) viii, Philadelphia, pp 40–52.

— 1992 'Early faunal evidence for dairying' in *Oxford Journal of Archaeology*, xi, pp 201– 9.

— 1992 'Exchange of livestock in Early Christian Ireland, AD 450–1150' in *Anthropozoologica*, xvi, pp 31–6.

— 1995 'Cows, ringforts and the origins of Early Christian Ireland' in *Emania*, xiii, pp 33–7.

McErlean, T. 1982 'The Early Christian settlement pattern and structure in west midAntrim', unpublished BA thesis, The Queen's University of Belfast.

McLeod, N. 1986 'Interpreting early Irish law: status and currency (part 1)' in *Zeitschrift fur Celtische Philologie*, xli, pp 46–65.

— 1987 'Interpreting early Irish law: status and currency (part 2)' in *Zeitschrift fur Celtische Philologie*, xlii, pp 41–115.

MacNeill, E. 1923 'Ancient Irish law: law of status and franchise' in *Proceedings of the Royal Irish Academy*, xxxvi, pp 265–316.

Mac Niocaill, G. 1971 'Tír Cumaile' in *Ériu*, xxii, pp 81–6.

Mallory, J. and McNeill, T. 1991 *The archaeology of Ulster*, Belfast.

Meitzen, A. 1895 *Siedelung und agranwesen der Westgermanen und Ostermanen der Kelten, Römer, Finnen und Slawen*, Berlin.

Meyer, K. (ed. and trans.) 1892 *Aislinge Meic Conglinne, The vision of Mac Conglinne*. London.

Mitchell, G.F. 1956 'Post-boreal pollen-diagrams from Irish raised-bogs' in *Proceedings of the Royal Irish Academy*, lvii, B, pp 185–251.

— 1965 'Littleton Bog, Tipperary: an Irish agricultural record' in *Journal of the Royal Society of Antiquaries of Ireland*, lcv, pp 121–32.

— 1986 *The Shell guide to reading the Irish landscape*. Dublin.

— and Tuite, B. 1993 *The great bog of Ardee*, Dundalk.

Monk, M. 1995 'A tale of two ringforts: Lisleagh I and II' in *Journal of the Cork Historical and Archaeological Society*, c, pp 105–16.

Moody, T., Martin, F. and Byrne, F. (eds) 1984 *A new history of Ireland; vol. ix, maps, genealogies, lists; a companion to Irish history, part ii*, Oxford.

Mount, C. 1995 'Excavations at Killanully, county Cork' in *Proceedings of the Royal Irish Academy*. xcv, C, pp 119–57.

Murphy, G. 1956 *Early Irish Lyrics: eighth to twelfth century*. Oxford.

Mytum, H. 1992 *The origins of Early Christian Ireland*. London.

Neihardt, J. 1989 *Black Elk speaks; being the life story of a holy man of the Oglala Sioux as told through John G. Neihardt (Flaming Rainbow)*, Lincoln, Nebraska.

Nicholls, K. 1984 'The land of the Leinstermen' in *Peritia*, iii, pp 535–58.

Ní Chatháin, P. and Richter, M. (ed.) 1984 *Ireland and Europe: the early church*. Stuttgart.

Nolan, W. and Hanigan, K. (ed.) 1994 *Wicklow: history and society*, Dublin.

O'Connell, M. 1991 'Vegetational and environmental changes in Ireland during the later Holocene' in O'Connell (comp.), *The post-glacial period (10,000–0 B.P.): fresh perspectives. Extended summaries of lectures.* Dublin, pp 21–5.

— (comp) 1991 *The post-glacial period (10,000–0 B.P.): fresh perspectives. Extended summaries of lectures* (Irish Association for Quaternary Studies). Dublin.

— (ed.) 1994 *Burren, Co. Clare* (Irish Association for Quaternary Studies, field guide no. 18). Dublin.

— 1994 'Ireland' in B. Frezel (ed.), *Evaluation of land surfaces cleared from forests in the Roman Iron Age and the time of migrating Germanic tribes based on regional pollen diagrams.* Stuttgart, pp 50–4.

— and Jelicic, L. 1994 'Lios Lairthín Mór (LLM II), N.W. Burren: history of vegetation and land use from 3200 B.P. to the present' in O'Connell (ed.), *Burren, Co. Clare*, pp 54–71.

— and Ni Ghrainne, E. 1994 'Inishbofin: palaeoecology' in Coxon and O'Connell (eds), *Clare Island and Inishbofin*. Dublin, pp 60–108.

O'Connor, M. 1944 'The excavation of three earthen ring-forts in the Liffey valley' in *Journal of the Royal Society of Antiquaries of Ireland*, lxxiv, pp 53–60.

Ó Corráin, D. (ed.) 1981 *Irish antiquity. Essays and studies presented to Professor M.J. O'Kelly.* Cork.

— 1983 'Some legal references to fences and fencing in Early Historic Ireland' in ReevesSmyth and Hamond (eds), *Landscape Archaeology*, pp 247–52.

Ó Cróinín, D. 1995 Early Medieval Ireland 400–1200. London.

Ó Cuileanáin, C. and Murphy, T. 1961 'A ringfort at Oldcourt, county Cork' in *Journal of the Cork Historical and Archaeological Society*, lxvi, pp 79–92.

O'Flaherty, B. 1982 'A locational analysis of the ringfort settlement of north county Kerry', unpublished M.A. thesis, University College Cork.

O'Flanagan, P. 1981 'Surveys, maps and the study of rural settlement development' in Ó Corráin (ed.) *Irish antiquity; essays and studies presented to Professor M.J. O'Kelly*, Cork, pp 320–6.

O'Grady, S. (ed. and trans.) 1892 *Silva Gadelica, (i–xxxi): A collection of tales in Irish with extracts illustrating persons and places.* London.

Ó Meara, J. (trans.) 1982 *The history and topography of Ireland*, London.

O'Hara, B. 1991 *The archaeological heritage of Killasser, county Mayo*, Galway.

O'Kelly, M. 1942 'A survey of antiquities in the barony of Small County, county Limerick; part I' in *North Munster Archaeological Journal*, iii, pp 75–97.

— 1942 'The excavation of a large earthen ring-fort at Garranes, county Cork' in *Proceedings of the Royal Irish Academy*, xlvii, C, pp 77–150.

— 1962 'Beal Boru, county Clare' in *Journal of the Cork Historical and Archaeological Society*, lxvii, pp 1–27.

— 1963 'Two ring-forts at Garryduff, Co. Cork' in *Proceedings of the Royal Irish Academy*, lxiii, C, pp 17–125.

— 1967 'Knockea, county Limerick' in E. Rynne (ed.), *North Munster studies: essays in commemoration of Monsignor Michael Moloney*, Limerick, pp 72–101.

Ó Riain, P. 1972 'Boundary association in Early Irish society' in *Studia Celtica*, vii, pp 12–29.

O'Sullivan, A. and J. Sheehan 1996 The Iveragh peninsula: an archaeological survey of south Kerry, Cork.

O'Sullivan, J. 1990 'The Lisnagun project' in Archaeology Ireland, iv, pp 23–5.

Ó Ríordáin, S. 1940 'Excavations at Cush, county Limerick' in *Proceedings of the Royal Irish Academy*, vi, C, pp 83–181.

— 1979 *Antiquities of the Irish countryside* (5th ed. revised by R. De Valera), London.

Patterson, N. 1994 *Cattle lords and clansmen: the social structures of Early Ireland*. 2nd ed. Notre Dame.

Plummer, C. (ed.) 1910 *Vitae Sanctorum Hiberniae*. Oxford.

— (ed. and trans.) 1922 *Bethada Náem nÉrenn* (2 vols), Oxford.

Proudfoot, V. 1957 'Settlement and economy in county Down from the late Bronze Age to the Anglo–Norman invasions', unpublished PhD thesis. The Queen's University of Belfast.

— 1959 'Note on a rath at Croft Road, Holywood, county Down' in *Ulster Journal of Archaeology*, xxii, pp 102–6.

— 1961 'The economy of the Irish rath' in *Medieval Archaeology*, v, pp 94–122.

Rackham, J. (ed.) 1994 *Environment and economy in Anglo-Saxon England*, York.

Raftery, J. 1944 'The Turoe Stone and the Rath of Feerwore' in *Journal of the Royal Society of Antiquaries of Ireland*, lxxiv, pp 23–52.

Reeves-Smyth, T. and Hamond, F. (eds) 1983 *Landscape Archaeology in Ireland*. Oxford.

Royal Irish Academy 1979 *Atlas of Ireland*, Dublin.

Ryan, M. 1973 'Native pottery in early historic Ireland' in *Proceedings of the Royal Irish Academy*, lxxiii, C, pp 619–45.

— (ed.) 1992 *The illustrated archaeology of Ireland*, Dublin.

Rynne, E. 1964 'Ringforts at Shannon airport' in *Proceedings of the Royal Irish Academy*, lxiii, C, pp 245–77.

— (ed.) 1967 *North Munster studies: essays in commemoration of Monsignor Michael Moloney*, Limerick.

Sharpe, R. 1991 *Medieval Irish saints' lives*. Oxford.

Simms, A. 1986 'Continuity and change: settlement and society in medieval Ireland *c*.500–1500' in W. Nolan (ed.), *The shaping of Ireland: the geographical perspective*, Cork, pp 44–65.

Sleeman, M. and Hurley, M. 1987 'Brownsbarn, county Dublin' in Cleary, Hurley and Twohig (eds), *Cork–Dublin gas pipeline*, Cork, pp 71–3.

Smyth, A. 1982 *Celtic Leinster; towards an historical geography of Early Irish civilisation A.D. 500–1600*, Dublin.

Speer, D. 1982 'The Early Christian settlement pattern in the south of the barony of Loughinsholin', unpublished BA thesis, The Queen's University of Belfast.

Stenberger, M. 1966 'A ring-fort at Raheennamadra, Knocklong, county Limerick' in *Proceedings of the Royal Irish Academy*, lxv, C, pp 37–54.

Stokes, W. (ed. and trans.) 1890 *Lives of the Saints from the Book of Lismore.* Oxford.

Stout, G. 1984 *Archaeological survey of the barony of Ikerrin.* Roscrea.

— et al., 1986–7 'The Sites and Monuments Record for county Wexford; an introduction' in *Journal of the Wexford Historical Society*, xi, pp 4–13.

— and Stout, M. 1992 'Patterns in the past: county Dublin 5000 BC–1000 AD' in Aalen and Whelan (eds), *Dublin*, pp 5–25.

— and Stout, M. 2011 'Early landscapes: from prehistory to Plantation' in F.H.A. Aalen, K. Whelan and M. Stout (eds), *Atlas of the Irish rural landscape*, Cork, pp 31–65.

Stout, M. 1989 'Ringforts in the south-west midlands', unpublished BA (mod.) dissertation. Trinity College Dublin.

— 1991 'Ringforts in the south–west midlands of Ireland' in *Proceedings of the Royal Irish Academy*, xci, C, pp 201–43.

— 1992 'Plans from plans: an analysis of the 1:2,500 OS series as a source for ringfort morphology', *Proceedings of the Royal Irish Academy*, XCII, C, pp 37–53.

— 1996 'Emyr Estyn Evans and Northern Ireland: the archaeology and geography of a new state' in Atkinson, Banks and O'Sullivan (eds) *Nationalism and archaeology*, Glasgow, pp 111–27.

— 1996 'Early Christian settlement and society in Ireland with particular reference to ringforts', unpublished PhD thesis, Trinity College Dublin.

— 1998 'Early Christian settlement, society and economy in Offaly' in W. Nolan and T.P. O'Neill (eds), *Offaly: History and society*, Dublin, pp 29–92.

— 2000 'Early Christian Ireland: settlement and environment' in T. Barry (ed.), *A history of settlement in Ireland*, London, pp 81–109.

— 2005 'Early Medieval boundaries' in T. Condit and C. Corlett (eds), *Above and beyond: essays in memory of Leo Swan*, Dublin, pp 139–48.

— 2012 'The distribution of Early Medieval ecclesiastical sites in Ireland' in P.J. Duffy and W. Nolan (eds), *At the anvil: essays in honour of William J. Smyth*, Dublin, pp 53–80.

— 2015 'The early medieval farm' in M. Murphy and M. Stout (eds), *Agriculture and settlement in Ireland*, Dublin, pp 14–27.

— 2015 'Early medieval settlement on Lough Ree' in B. Cunningham and H. Murtagh (eds), *Lough Ree: historic lakeland settlement*, Dublin, 70–82.

— 2017 *Early Medieval Ireland 431–1169*, Dublin.

Swan, L. 1983 'Enclosed ecclesiastical sites and their relevance to settlement patterns of the first millennium A.D.' in Reeves–Smyth and Hamond (eds) *Landscape archaeology*, pp 269–94.

— 1988 'The Early Christian ecclesiastical sites of county Westmeath' in J. Bradley (ed.), *Settlement and society in Medieval Ireland; studies presented to F.X. Martin*, Kilkenny, pp 3–32.

Thomas, C. 1959 'Imported pottery in Dark-Age western Britain' in *Medieval Archaeology*, iii, pp 89–111.

Toal, C. 1995 *North Kerry archaeological survey*, Dingle.

Warner, R. 1988 'The archaeology of early historic Irish kingship', in Driscoll and Nieke (eds), *Power and politics*, pp 47–68.

Waterman, D. 1955 'Excavations at Seafin castle and Ballyroney motte and bailey' in *Ulster Journal of Archaeology*, xviii, pp 83–104.

— 1963 'Excavations at Duneight, county Down' in *Ulster Journal of Archaeology*, xxvi, pp 55–78.

Watson, E. 1940 'Prehistoric sites in south Antrim' in *Ulster Journal of Archaeology*, iii, pp 142–51.

Weir, D. 1995 'A palynological study of landscape and agricultural development in county Louth from the second millennium BC to the first millennium AD' in *Discovery Programme reports 2; project results 1993*, Dublin, pp 77–126.

Westropp, T. 1902 'The ancient forts of Ireland: being a contribution towards our knowledge of their types, affinities and structural features', in *Transactions of the Royal Irish Academy*, xxxi, pp 579–730.

Whelan, K. (ed.) 1987 *Wexford: history and society*, Dublin.

Williams, B. 1984 'Excavations at Ballyutoag, county Antrim' in *Ulster Journal of Archaeology*, xlvii, pp 37–49.

Williams, B. 1985 'Excavation of a rath at Coolcran, county Fermanagh' in *Ulster Journal of Archaeology*, xlviii, pp 69–79.

Wood, T. 1821 *An inquiry concerning the primitive inhabitants of Ireland*. Cork.